UKRAINIAN SUNRISE

STORIES OF THE DONETSK AND LUHANSK
REGIONS FROM THE EARLY 2000S

Ukrainian Studies

Series Editor: Vitaly Chernetsky (University of Kansas)

Other Titles in this Series:

UKRAINIAN SUNRISE

STORIES OF THE DONETSK AND LUHANSK REGIONS FROM THE EARLY 2000S

KATERYNA ZAREMBO

TRANSLATED FROM UKRAINIAN
BY TETIANA SAVCHYNSKA

ACADEMIC STUDIES PRESS
BOSTON
2024

Library of Congress Control Number: 2024947377

ISBN 9798887197050 (hardback)
ISBN 9798887197067 (paperback)
ISBN 9798887197074 (ebook Adobe PDF)
ISBN 9798887197081 (ePub)

Book design by Lapiz Digital Services

On the cover: Alla Horska, a sketch for the mosaic panel
"The Coal Flower," for the "Krasnodonvuhillia" Administrative Building,
1968 (Sorokyne [Krasnodon until 2016] in Luhansk region;
temporarily occupied by Russia since 2014). Reproduced by permission.

Published by Academic Studies Press
1007 Chestnut st., Newton MA, 02464, USA
press@academicstudiespress.com
www.academicstudiespress.com

This book has been published with the support of the Translate Ukraine Program

UKRAINIAN
//IIIBOOK
INSTITUTE

To the memory of my grandpa, Viktor Horodetskyi,
who showed me what it means to be principled

Contents

Translator's Acknowledgements

———

First and foremost, I want to thank Kateryna Zarembo, who entrusted me with translating her book. It has been a great honor for me, an intellectual challenge, and a big responsibility. I would also like to express my deepest gratitude to my friends and colleagues: Nina Murray, the first reader of this translation, for her encouragement and guidance, and Teresa Pearce for having generously read drafts of the entire manuscript and for providing valuable feedback and suggestions. Finally, I am immensely grateful to my sister, Olya Walden, for her unrelenting support and profound belief in me and my work.

To pretend that Ukrainian Donbas doesn't exist is to commit a crime.

—*Stanislav Fedorchuk*

Once you begin learning the history of the Donetsk region, you quickly become a patriot.

—*Fr. Vasyl Ivaniuk*

Preface

The Ukrainian East: Forget Everything (You Thought) You Knew about Donbas

———

This manuscript was supposed to be completed in early March 2022. On February 24th, I had one of my last scheduled interviews. But Russia's full-scale invasion put the work on hold indefinitely.

In early April, I received a call from the publisher.

"Katia, how's the book coming along?"

I mumbled something incoherent in response—"Who needs it now?" or something along those lines.

"Keep writing. People need a sense of normality."

It wasn't so much that people really do need a normality in which there is a space for reading and paper books—I'm sure that everyone who couldn't bring themselves to read after February 24 felt this thirst for reading, because it turned out that reading books was not a luxury but one of the basic needs that invigorate the mind and spirit, even (or especially) in the midst of the hardest of times, or that this conversation restored my normality—the work on the book that had been ongoing, with pauses and breaks, since 2017—and my sense of purpose.

It was that the Ukrainian Donbas—or, more appropriately, the Ukrainian Donetsk and Luhansk regions—are as much of a normality as the Ukrainian Kherson, Volyn, or Chernihiv regions.[1] And if some find it difficult to accept

---

1 Here "region" is used to denote "oblast", an administrative territorial unit of Ukraine. If "the region" is used without a proper noun, it stands for "an area".

this, that's only because, for many Ukrainians, their knowledge of the Donetsk and Luhansk regions is still shaped by imperial—Russian, Soviet, post-Soviet—narratives. This book is an attempt to decolonize this knowledge. You will see the Donetsk and Luhansk regions you are not used to. A Donbas that Russia would rather you didn't know about.

***

Ukraine's East—or, more precisely, the part of it that has come to be labeled "Donbas"—is perhaps the most mythologized and demonized Ukrainian region. Donbas is shrouded in scores of myths and stereotypes that originated with the Soviet government and were then continued and reinforced by the local political elite in independent Ukraine.

Donbas—Russian-speaking, pro-Russian, a land of miners, oligarchic clans and criminals, a submissive proletariat that votes for the local "tsar" as ordered, and finally, an absolute fiefdom of the Party of Regions—is a long way from the exhaustive list of stereotypical ideas about the region that have been imposed systematically and fairly successfully throughout Ukraine. Given the lack of well-developed regional studies in Ukraine in general (how much do we know about the history, identity, and regional peculiarities of, say, Polissia or Pokuttia?) and "Donbas studies" in particular, most people accepted these stereotypes at face value. The spread of these stereotypes turned out to be so successful that a university professor from Donetsk could be asked, half-jokingly and half-seriously, whether he or his wife had a criminal past because "every other person in Donbas has been in prison."[2] Since 2004, the demonization of Donbas has intensified: "For residents of other regions, the local population went from being people from the Donetsk region to 'donetski' or 'those from Donetsk' in a matter of days."[3] In 2014, all existing stereotypes were compounded by the stigma of separatism, to the extent that some people were unwilling to rent out apartments to internally displaced persons (IDPs) of both the first (2014) and second (2022) waves who were registered as living in Donetsk or Luhansk.

There is no doubt that the Party of Regions and the local oligarchy, who effectively monopolized the "voice" of Donbas for almost twenty years from the late '90s until the beginning of Russian aggression in 2014, played a significant role in shaping the region's image, highlighting its alleged distinctiveness. The

---

2 Marta Shokalo, "Donbas—shakhtars'kyi krai" [Donbas—a miner's land], BBC News Ukraine, December 22, 2009, https://www.bbc.com/ukrainian/ukraine/2009/12/091222_donbass_one_marta_sp.

3 Olha Klinova, "Oksana Mikheieva: Iak formuvalas' rehional'na identychnist' Donbasu" [Oksana Mikheieva: How the regional identity of Donbas was formed], *Istorychna pravda*, December 11, 2014, https://www.istpravda.com.ua/articles/2014/12/11/146063/.

region became strongly associated with organized crime and criminals, fueled by regular news about criminal charges: fifty-seven kingpins of the criminal world were killed in Donbas from the mid-1990s to the mid-2000s.[4] It was also associated with being Russian-speaking and "regionalists" (and/or "those from Donetsk"), even to the point of outright demonization—it's worth recalling the Russian-language slogan of Yushchenko's local campaign headquarters, "We defeated Nazism, we will defeat the 'donetski,'"[5] as well as the Russian-language neologisms of mass public discourse, such as "Thank you, people of Donbas, for the president[6] who's f**ked us up the ass."[7]

In a bitter irony, another slogan, "To Hear Donbas," actually took away the voice of those residents whose identity, activities, and narratives did not conform to the image created by the local political elite. Before 2014, there had been isolated attempts to show "another" Donbas, such as *Solomon's Red Star*, a collection of essays about twenty-five regions of Ukraine[8] in which the poet Lyubov Yakimchuk and the historian Stanislav Fedorchuk wrote about the Luhansk and Donetsk regions respectively. In the clash of narratives, however, the balance of power was too uneven.

It could also be argued that the remoteness of the East from other regions of Ukraine—not so much geographical as mental—also contributed to this pattern. No wonder Donbas is sometimes referred to as the "Far East"[9] (as Yuriy Pokalchuk and Mykola Riabchuk, among others, have called it), although in reality it is not that remote: the distance between Kyiv and Donetsk exceeds the distance between Kyiv and Lviv by only 150 kilometers. Nevertheless, people in Donbas itself compare the region to an island.[10]

---

4 Volodymyr Bilets'kyi, "Skhid Ukrainy v intehrativnykh protsesakh suchasnogo derzhavot-vorennia" [Ukraine's East in the integrative processes of modern state formation], http://www.experts.in.ua/baza/analitic/index.php?ELEMENT_ID=10955.

5 Cited from Andrii Portnov, "Svoboda ta vybir na Donbasi" [Freedom and choice in Donbas], *Krytyka* 3 (2005): 5–6.

6 A reference to Viktor Yanukovych, who hails from the region (translator's note).

7 Andrii Portnov has already pointed out the "internal orientalism" that some observers have used to describe Ukraine's East as not only different, but worse. See: Andrii Portnov, "Ukraina ta ii 'dalekyi skhid.' Pro h aly ts'kyi reduktsionizm ta ioho henealohiiu" [Ukraine and its "far east." On Galician reductionism and its genealogy], Historians.in.ua, August 1, 2014, http://www.historians.in.ua/index.php/en/avtorska-kolonka/1231-andrii-portnov-ukraina-ta-ii-dalekyi-skhid-pro-halytskyi-reduktsionizm-ta-ioho-henealohiiu.

8 Published by Tempora Publishing in 2012.

9 Bohdan Butkevych, "Literaturni povstantsi Dalekoho Skhodu" [Literary rebels of the far east], *Ukrains'kyi tyzhden'*, May 14, 2010, https://tyzhden.ua/literaturni-povstantsi-dalekoho-skhodu/.

10 Tetiana Levonyuk, "Ostannii forpost Donbasu" [The last outpost of Donbas], *New Europe Center*, June 14, 2019, http://neweurope.org.ua/analytics/ostannij-forpost-donbasu/.

It is isolation that has become the metaphor defining the modern history of Donbas: the Donetsk art center Izolyatsia, which was intended to overcome the cultural and artistic isolation of the region as a channel for contemporary art to the easternmost outpost of Europe, was only open for four years before being turned into a prison and torture camp of the so-called "Donetsk People's Republic" (DPR).[11] Once again, isolation turned from metaphorical to literal.

The region's loneliness within the state (even before 2014) was so pronounced that even some Ukrainian intellectuals bought into the myth of a pro-Russian Donbas,[12] thereby offending those in the East who were fond of them and their work. Meanwhile, the work of pro-Ukrainian organizations and movements over the period of Ukrainian independence remains under-researched.

However, even a cursory overview reveals numerous cultural and civic organizations that had been operating in Donetsk and Luhansk since 1991 and up until the Russian invasion of 2014, and that could be considered the beginnings of a national revival.

These are the communities that I want to talk about in this book.

***

In this book, I write about Ukrainian communities and movements in Donetsk and Luhansk regions that existed between the 2000s and 2014. At some point, I realized that I was writing mostly about my peers, the generation born in the 1980s, whose childhood and teenage years were spent in an independent Ukraine.

I would like to note that this is the second generation of Ukrainian patriots from Donetsk and Luhansk in the period of independence. The 1990s were marked by different names and organizations: The Taras Shevchenko Ukrainian Language Society, the Prosvita chapter, the RUKH NGO, the Kalmius Palanka of the Ukrainian Cossacks, the Kurin Historical and Ethnographic Society, and other communities and societies.

---

11 Since 2014, the Izolyatsia Foundation, a platform for cultural initiative, has been operating in Kyiv at the following address: 12 Naberezhno-Luhova St. Its website is https://izolyatsia. org/en/.

12 There is a well-known 2010 interview with Yuriy Andrukhovych in which he suggested allowing Crimea and Donbas to break away. Later, the writer claimed that he had partially changed his views. Yuriy Andrukhovych, "Iakshcho peremozhut' pomaranchevi, to Krymu i Donbasu treba dati mozhlyvist' vidokremytysia" [If the 'Orange' win, Crimes and Donbas should be allowed to break away], UNIAN, July 22, 2010, https://www.unian.ua/politics/382762-andruhovich-yakscho-peremojut-pomaranchevi-to-krimu-y-donbasu-treba-dati-mojlivist-vidokremitisya.html.

The list could go on. The historian Oksana Mikheieva, a Donetsk native who lived and worked there for many years, recalls how in 1989, she sewed the national flags of all the Soviet republics at home, and her activist friends later took them to a May Day demonstration. In November 1991, the Donetsk State Academic *Russian* (sic! Italics mine—K.Z.) Opera and Ballet Theater staged a play to raise funds for the Kyiv-Mohyla Academy Renaissance Foundation— even before the University's first students in independence-era Ukraine began their studies there.

Ukrainian movements in the Donetsk and Luhansk regions were a systemic rather than a sporadic phenomenon.

***

I came across these stories one after another: Yuriy Matushchak and Poshtovkh, the local community of Muslims and their patriotism toward Ukraine, *The Aeneid* in the village of Oleksandro-Kalynove in the Donetsk region, the history and philology departments at Vasyl Stus Donetsk National University, the Luhansk art association STAN, and the Euromaidans in Donetsk and Luhansk. And every time I came across a new story, I was thrilled: "Wow! Wow! Wow!" This would be followed by a pang of shame. If Donbas is Ukraine, then why do Ukrainian movements, communities, and events surprise me as if I were discovering rose bushes down coal mines? A myth one has gotten used to has a way of persisting.

***

I do not intend for this text to be exhaustive. On the contrary: there are too many Ukrainian movements and communities in the Ukrainian East to cover them all in one book. Many of them were not covered in this research: for example, the stories of Plast in the Donetsk region, the contemporary Cossack and human rights movements, ecoactivists, some religious denominations, as well as some big stories about the work of political parties (Svoboda and other parties had chapters in Donbas; even in the local government there were those who sided with pro-Ukrainian forces, openly or covertly) and business circles in the Donetsk and Luhansk regions.

***

This is a very one-sided book. It's about just one side of Donbas. A real side, and yet just one of many. I wouldn't want you to think, after reading this book, that this is the whole of Donbas. It is the real Donbas, but it's not the whole of it. Here is a quote from Serhiy Zhadan that best explains the diversity of Donbas:

What did my trips to Donbas show me? Hundreds of people came to my readings and concerts. At some point each of them had accepted their Ukrainian identity almost as people accept a new religion, even if that may sound overly dramatic. They were slowly reclaiming themselves.

There shouldn't be any illusions about whether this is the true Donbas. On the contrary, it should highlight the fact that Donbas is not homogenous.

It would be an incredible simplification to reduce everything to a single concept.[13]

The same can be said of the people featured in my book. Their stories might be somewhat romantic, but I would not like to idealize them—neither the people, nor their stories. Donbas, just like the rest of Ukraine, is home to ordinary people: mostly, but not exclusively Ukrainians; heroes and antiheroes; prominent and "average"; in short, just like everyone else.

***

This research spans a wide geographical area, reflecting the so-called "dispersion" of Donbas across Ukraine: after 2014, the majority of those who supported the Ukrainian idea in Donbas became internally displaced people and moved to Kyiv, Vinnytsia, Uzhhorod, Lviv, Dnipro, Kharkiv, Ivano-Frankivsk, Irpin, and other Ukrainian cities. I find this situation a kind of metaphor for the role of Donbas in Ukraine after the war broke out: while the Ukrainian state lost control over a part of the eastern territories, it also got to know the East better—at least through its former residents who suddenly became neighbors of people who lived in Kharkiv, Vinnytsia, Kyiv, Lviv, etc. And so, in addition to traveling to the East, I also recorded interviews in Kyiv, Uzhhorod, Ivano-Frankivsk, Vinnytsia, and other cities, both in person and online.

The genre of this book—non-fiction or documentary prose, based on many oral histories—opens up opportunities for the researcher but also imposes limitations. On the one hand, this method allows for many real voices to be heard and their unique experience to be conveyed. On the other hand, the reproduction of personal experience passes through a double filter—the perception of

---

13 Serhiy Zhadan, "If We Don't Want to Separate Off the East, We Need to Get to Know It," in Oleksandr Mykhed, *I'll Mix Your Blood with Coal: Snapshots from the East of Ukraine*, trans. Tetiana Savchynska and David Mossop (Evanston: Northwestern University Press, 2025).

the person who lived through it and the perception of the person telling the story (me as the narrator). One of my interviewees put it this way: "This is just my interpretation. But I think it approximates the truth."

This book is my interpretation of the Ukrainian Donetsk and Luhansk regions the way I read, heard, and saw them. But I think it approximates the truth.

***

I am grateful to Serhiy Stukanov, who wrote a Facebook post about Ukrainian movements in the Donetsk region back in 2016. His post inspired me to write this book.

My sincere gratitude to Stanislav Fedorchuk, whom I consider the godfather of this book. I don't know anyone else who has worked so tirelessly to educate as many people as possible about the Ukrainian East. Stanislav was generous in sharing stories, contacts, and sources with me, and most importantly, he immediately believed me and in me, and that faith kept me going every time.

I would like to thank all the interviewees who shared their experience and knowledge with me. In particular, I am sincerely grateful to Dmytro Bilko, Oleksandr Biletskyi, Fr. Ihnatiy Volovenko, Mykhailo Hlybokyi, Oleksandr Demchenko, Petro Dudnyk, Fr. Vasyl Ivaniuk, Said Ismagilov, Tetiana Zarovna, Serhiy Zlyvko, Volodymyr Kipen, Valeriy Kravchenko, Oleksiy Matsuka, Yaroslav Minkin, Yevhen Monastyrskyi, Maksym Potapchuk, Kostiantyn Reutskyi, Vitaliy Rudenkyi, Yevhen Nasadyuk, Bohdan Novak, Vitaliy Ovcharenko, Leonid Samofalov, Serhiy Stukanov, Olena Stiazhkina, Andriy Taraman, Ihor Todorov, Yuriy Temirov, Oleksiy Chupa, Kateryna Yakovlenko, and those who wished to remain anonymous.

I am equally grateful to the reviewers, Oksana Mikheieva and Yevhen Hlibovytskyi, who read the entire book, and to Ihor Kozlovskyi and Mykhailo Yakubovych, who reviewed the chapter on religious communities. Any mistakes and oversights are my sole responsibility.

I am grateful to Choven Publishing, and specifically to Ihor Balynskyi and Yuriy Opoka, for instantly believing in my idea. I see an obvious symbolism in the fact that a book about the Ukrainian East is being released by a Lviv publisher.

I am grateful to the Kharkiv office of the Konrad Adenauer Stiftung, especially to Oleksiy Leznov and Brigitta Triebel, for supporting this research. Their support came just at the right time and when I least expected it. My collaboration with this foundation, which came about as a result of a series of magical coincidences, was a gift from fate and a confirmation that writing this book was important.

I am grateful to Yaroslav Yasenets for transcribing the recordings of my interviews. I believe that our acquaintance and cooperation in this project were no accident.

I am grateful to my parents, Valeriy and Halyna Zarembo, for never having any expectations of me other than to follow my heart.

I am infinitely grateful to my husband, Yuriy, my most attentive listener and conversation partner—he was the first person I shared my ideas and findings with; it was in conversations with him that I found the exact words and language. I would also like to thank him for his constant support—he has always encouraged me to move forward despite my doubts—and, of course, for spending time with our four children, giving me space for research and reflection. Finally, my deepest gratitude to the nanny of my children, Nataliya Prots—a big (the biggest) share of my work rests on her shoulders.

Kyiv, August 2022

Chapter 1

The Myth of Donbas: An Attempt at Deconstruction

The term "Donbas" has become so ingrained in contemporary Ukrainian and foreign discourse that it is considered virtually synonymous with the Donetsk and Luhansk regions. "The first blue-and-yellow flag in Donbas was raised in Bakhmut," the website of the Donetsk Regional State Administration states.[1] "Volodymyr Zelenskyi arrives in Donbas,"[2] a headline on the website of the President's Office reads on October 14, 2021. The Izolyatsia Art Foundation, which moved from Donetsk to Kyiv in 2014, calls one of its projects dedicated to the study of the Ukrainian East "Donbas Studies." A collection of literary works by writers from Donetsk and Luhansk regions is titled *A Rock: An Anthology of Ukrainian Writers of Donbas*. The term "Donbas" is used in academic discourse as well: a collective monograph edited by Viktor Kotyhorenko, and published by the Ivan Kuras Institute of Political and Ethnic Studies at the National

---

1 Donetsk Regional State Administration, "Z istorii ukrainskoho Donbasu: Bakhmut—pershe misto na Donechchyni, iake pidnialo syn'o-zhovtyi stiah" [From the history of Ukrainian Donbass: Bakhmut—the first city in Donetsk region to raise a blue and yellow flag], August 23, 2020, https://dn.gov.ua/galleries/z-istoriyi-ukrayinskogo-donbasu-bahmut-pershe-misto-na-donechchini-yake-pidnyalo-sino-zhovtij-styag.

2 President of Ukraine's official website, "Volodymyr Zelens'kyi prybuv na Donbas" [Volodymyr Zelenskyi arrives in Donbas], October 14, 2021, https://www.president.gov.ua/news/volodimir-zelenskijpribuv-na-donbas-71093.

Academy of Sciences of Ukraine, is titled "Donbas in the Ethnological and Political Dimensions." And this list could go on and on. Even leading sociological agencies and think tanks use the term "Donbas" to refer to the macro-region comprising the Donetsk and Luhansk regions.[3] As for academic publications and media articles where "Donbas" is defined as a toponym synonymous with the Donetsk and Luhansk regions, a list of them in this work would be endless and unnecessary.

The Russian invasion of the region sparked considerable research and public interest in Donbas. This resulted in the publication of books and articles meant to shed light on the essence of the region in a balanced way. The most well-known and comprehensive of these were *I'll Mix Your Blood with Coal: Snapshots from the East of Ukraine* by Oleksandr Mykhed (Nash Format Publishing, 2020), *The Wild East. An Account of Donbas's Past and Present* by Maksym Vikhrov (Tempora Publishing, 2018), *Three Hundred Years of Solitude: A Ukrainian Donbas in Search of Meaning and Homeland* by Stanislav Kulchytskyi and Larysa Yakubova (Clio Publishing, 2016), and *Ukrainian Donbas: The Faces of Regional Identity* by Marta Studenna-Skrukwa (The Laboratory for Legislative Initiatives, 2014). It's worth noting that the toponym "Donbas" or its equivalents are often accompanied by the descriptor "Ukrainian"[4]—as though the identity of this region attracted the authors as an unsolved mystery, not as something self-explanatory. It seemed almost as if there were another, non-Ukrainian Donbas—after all, it would hardly occur to anyone to discuss the "Ukrainianness" of the Zhytomyr, Odesa, or Podillia regions in the same vein.

At the same time, some Ukrainian intellectuals—representatives of the region—warn against using this word. "Donbas Will Not Return to Ukraine Because Donbas Does Not Exist" is the title of a famous talk by Olena Stiazhkina, a historian from Donetsk, delivered at TEDxKyiv in 2014.[5] In her talk, Stiazhkina explains, "The word 'Donbas' doesn't define anything. When

---

3   For example, the Ilko Kucheriv Democratic Initiatives Foundation, "Donbas: Komunikatsiia ta kontakty z meshkantsiamy tymchasovo nepidkontrol'nykh terytorii" [Donbas: Communication and Contacts with the Residents of the Territories Temporarily Not Controlled by Ukraine], August 10, 2017, https://dif.org.ua/article/donbas-komunikatsiya-ta-kontakti-z-meshkantsyami-timchasovonepidkontrolnikh-teritoriy.

4   For instance, Stanislav Kul'chyts'kyi and Larysa Iakubova, *Trysta rokiv samotnosti: Ukrains'kyi Donbas u poshukakh smysliv i Bat'kivshchyny* [Three hundred years of solitude: A Ukrainian Donbas in search of meaning and homeland] (Kyiv: Klio, 2016); or Marta Studenna-Skrukwa, *Ukrains'ky i Donbas: Oblychchia rehional'noi identychnosti* [Ukrainian Donbas: The faces of regional identity] (Kyiv: Laboratoriia zakonodavchykh initsiatyv, 2014).

5   Olena Stiazhkina, "Donbas ne povernet'sia v Ukrainu, bo Donbasu ne isnuie" [Donbas will not return to Ukraine because Donbas does not exist], *Ukrains'ka pravda*, November 3, 2014, https://www.pravda.com.ua/columns/2014/11/3/7043067/.

we say 'Donbas,' it's equivalent to us reading a Russian-language poem by Yuz Aleshkovsky: 'Comrade Stalin, may you live a thousand years; and even if I have to die in the taiga, the country will have more iron and steel per capita.'" Ihor Kozlovskyi, a Ukrainian religion studies scholar from Donetsk who spent seven hundred days in captivity in the so-called "Donetsk People's Republic," shares a similar opinion: "Donbas is an economic and relative term; you cannot call all of this Donbas."[6]

Initially, the term "Donbas" (short for the Donetsk Coal Basin), which was coined in the nineteenth century by a Russian engineer, Yevgraf Kovalevsky, referred to an industrial region whose territory didn't correspond to the present-day borders of Donetsk and Luhansk regions. The industrial region included part of the Donetsk region without Pryazovia (the southeastern region of Ukraine located on the shores of the Sea of Azov), the south of the Luhansk region, the east of the Dnipropetrovsk region, and the west of Russia's Rostov region, which means that part of Donbas as a coal basin is located within Russia's borders. That's why Hiroaki Kuromiya, in his book *Freedom and Terror in the Donbas: The Ukrainian–Russian Borderlands, 1870s–1990s*, uses the term "Donbas" correctly—Kuromiya was indeed referring only to the mining and borderland area of the region.[7]

The Ukrainian intellectuals' reservations are not, however, caused by the fact that the name of the Donetsk coal basin has become synonymous with the Donetsk and Luhansk regions within their administrative borders. After all, words acquiring new meanings over time is a natural phenomenon in any language, and in the case of Donbas it could have been harmless (another example of the same phenomenon is the name "Galicia," or *Halychyna*, which refers to the Lviv, Ternopil, and Ivano-Frankivsk regions). It is unlikely that the politicians, researchers, and journalists mentioned above, when using the term "Donbas" to refer to the region, intended the term to have industrial and economic, rather than administrative and territorial semantics. Moreover, there's no alternative to this toponym in the Ukrainian language: the term "East" is too broad, as it usually includes the Kharkiv region as well.

Rather, what draws criticism is the use of the term "Donbas" in the sense artificially created by the Soviet myth, and Stiazhkina's quote above refers to that myth.

***

---

6 Cited in Mykhed, *I'll Mix Your Blood with Coal*, 79.
7 Hiroaki Kuromiya, *Freedom and Terror in the Donbas: A Ukrainian-Russian Borderland, 1870s-1990s* (Cambridge: Cambridge University Press, 2003).

In a word, Donbas is fiction.

The Donetsk coal basin was of strategic importance for the Soviet government: it's worth recalling Vladimir Lenin's famous quote: "Donbas [. . .] is a region without which the building of socialism will remain merely a good intention" (this phrase was engraved on the monument to Lenin erected in Donetsk in 1967). The region was too important for the Soviet Union to tolerate its Ukrainian identity. And not only Ukrainian identity: the Soviet myth of Donbas as an "All-Union furnace" not only rejected other identities, it also denied their very existence, except for heavy industry workers. "The evil power of the myth of Donbas is that a huge number of people excluded from it have been in the zone of invisibility. These people are intellectuals, peasants, women, and children. And also Ukrainians, along with any other nationalities except for the "great Russian (Soviet) people."[8]

The myth of Donbas also denied the region its own history, portraying it as a *tabula rasa* that exists only because of and for the sake of the Soviet sheaves of wheat. At the same time, the continuity of Sovietism remained after the restoration of independence: it's no coincidence that the Communist Party of Ukraine was established in Donetsk in 1993, which is why researcher Maria Karmazina calls the city "the birthplace of communism" in independent Ukraine. In 2015, the Donetsk and Luhansk regions ranked first and second, respectively, in terms of the number of cities and towns that were to be renamed under the new decommunization law[9] (ten cities and eleven towns in the Donetsk region, six cities and thirteen towns in the Luhansk region).[10] The situation with local toponyms—streets, boulevards, avenues, lanes, etc.—was even worse. According to Yevhen Shybalov, 1,350 toponyms in the region are associated with the Soviet period. Lenin was mentioned 430 times, Kirov 67 times, Kalinin 57 times, Shchors 43 times, Artem 33 times, etc.[11] According to Fedorchuk, the imperial interpretation of the "Wild Fields" was aimed at "reducing the rights of the indigenous population and the Zaporizhzhian Army to these lands to zero."[12] But in

---

8 Ibid.

9 Mariia Karmazina, *Politychni identychnosti v suchasnii Ukraini: miska hromada Donetska.* [Political identities in modern Ukraine: Donetsk urban community] (Kyiv: Instytut politychnykh i etnonatsional'nykh doslidzhen' imeni I. F. Kurasa Natsional'noi akademii nauk Ukrainy, 2016), 122–123.

10 The third region on the list was Crimea.

11 Evgenii Shybalov, "Donbasskoe identity: neukrainskaia Ukraina" [Donbass identity: Non-Ukrainian Ukraine], *Zerkalo nedeli*, December 21, 2007, http://gazeta.zn.ua/POLITICS/donbasskoe_identity__neukrainskaya_ukraina.html.

12 Stanislav Fedorchuk, "Rozpiznavannia Donbasu" [Recognizing Donbas], *Poshtovkh* 1 (December 2008): 4.

reality, the history of the region is much deeper, and in the public consciousness, this area should have been a part of the Cossack myth because its territory was part of the Zaporizhzhian Sich, and the Donetsk region was part of the Kalmius Palanka.[13] The name of Druzhkivka, a town in the northern Donetsk region, comes from the Cossack history of the area. Another town, Yasynuvata, used to be a Cossack settlement. The villages of Volodarske and Boiove were founded by the Cossacks in Pryazovia. The Kalmius Palanka had up to 60 winter quarters (Cossack settlements), and the Luhansk Palanka had about 13.[14]

Finally, the myth of Donbas deliberately erases the peculiarities of the region at the micro level and portrays it as a homogeneous whole. In fact, residents of the region would be the first to say that "Donbas" and "the Donetsk and Luhansk regions" are not synonymous. "What do the Milovsky, Markovsky, Novopskov, Bilokurakine, Starobilsk, Bilovodsk, Novoaydar, Troitsk, Svatovo, and Kremmina districts of the Luhansk region have to do with Donbas?" asks Ihor Sayenko, a historian from Luhansk. "All of these districts and the western part of the Stanychno-Luhansk district, which were located north of the Siverskyi Donets River, were and still are purely agricultural. There have never been any mines here, or coal industry enterprises."[15] In Svatove, which belongs to the historic region of Slobozhanshchyna, the locals don't even know when Miners' Day is.[16] "This isn't Donbas, this is Pryazovia," residents of Mariupol will tell you.

The Donetsk and Luhansk regions are very different—from each other, and within themselves.

What the Mines Hide

Since the Soviet myth of Donbas revolves around its heavy industry, creating an "artificial 'halo of glory'" around the work of metallurgists and miners, along with the system of rewards, distribution of housing and necessities based on

---

13 Kalmius Palanka was one of the eight palankas (administrative-territorial units) of the Lower Zaporizhzhian Army of the New Sich (1734–1775).

14 Maksym Vikhrov, *Dykyi skhid. Narys istorii ta s'ohodennia Donbasu* [Wild east. Sketches on the past and present of Donbas] (Kyiv: Tempora, 2018), 20–21.

15 Ihor Saienko, "Donbas i Luhanshchyna—dvi velyki riznytsi" [The Donbas and Luhansk regions are very different], *Istorychna pravda*, August 29, 2012, https://www.istpravda.com.ua/columns/2012/08/29/92563/.

16 "Pochemu Svatovu udalos' dat' otpor separatizmu? [Why did Svatove manage to resist separatism?], *Donbas. Realii*, February 17, 2017, https://www.radiosvoboda.org/a/28316111.html.

"labor performance," as well as "an atmosphere of patriotic fervor,"[17] this part of the myth deserves special attention. Miners' salaries were among the highest in the Soviet Union, and the older generation of Donetsk residents still recall that the region was second only to Moscow and Leningrad in terms of food supply. Ironically, a mine also became a "window to Europe," if not for the miners themselves, then at least for their children, who were the first among their peers in the Soviet Union to own a personal stereo and a pair of jeans.[18] The region's sporting glory was achieved by the Shakhtar and Metallurg soccer teams.

The truth is, the mining industry has been inefficient and unprofitable since at least the 1960s. "In the mid-1970s, more than 40% of coal in Donbas was mined from the layers up to 1.2 meters high, which were not mined anywhere else in the world because of their unprofitability.[19] Safety measures were virtually non-existent, equipment was outdated, coal quality was poor, and mine accidents were commonplace. In 1989, with 2.5 million workers, the Soviet coal industry produced 800 million tonnes of coal, whereas just 140,000 American miners produced 1 billion tonnes of coal, and of much higher quality.[20]

Even the famed Soviet labor heroes turned out to be fictional characters. Alexei Stakhanov was a participant in a specially orchestrated performance by the Soviet authorities under the supervision of the mine's chief engineer that was conducted in gross violation of safety procedures.[21] The famed metallurgist Nikita Izotov was, in fact, a drunkard and a brawler.[22]

The "miner's myth" began to fade in the late Soviet period, especially for the locals—for them, the mine began to lose its appeal in the 1980s. For the region's young people, mining was the last resort when it came to choosing a career ("If there's nothing else I'm good at, I'll go work at a mine").[23]

In independent Ukraine, the "miner's myth" and the cult of physical strength were propped up by the regional authorities. The regional miner's identity was deliberately fueled more than the Ukrainian national identity: one example

---

17 Iaroslava Vermenych, *Donbas iak porubizhnyi rehion: terytorialnyi vymir* [Donbas as a border region: The territorial dimension] (Kyiv: Instytut istorii Ukrainy Natsional'noi akademii nauk Ukrainy, 2015), 22.

18 Volodymyr Prykhod'ko, "Identichnost' Donbassa: Istoriia odnogo filosofa" [The identity of Donbass: A story of a philosopher], https://studway.com.ua/volodymyr-pryhodko/?fbclid=IwAR2enA6wiOlU_hMc5UewWC4CAVvbzxXnh8CYPctOeTxJ2EkWk3W3zxXzlQ.

19 Vikhrov, *Dykyi skhid*, 197.

20 Ibid., 221.

21 The incident is described in detail ibid., 150–154.

22 Klinova, "Iak formuvalasia."

23 That's how Olena Stiazhkina recalled the mood among young people in the 1980s in her conversation with Oleksandr Mykhed (*I'll Mix Your Blood with Coal*, 269).

of this is the celebration of Miners' Day on the last Sunday of August, which was much more joyous than Ukraine's Independence Day on August 24. For the Euro 2012 Championship, the slogan "Donetsk—Strength and Beauty" was illustrated with images of coal and roses, traditional symbols of Donetsk. The Party of Regions broadcast the motto "Donbas Feeds the Whole of Ukraine" throughout the country, emphasizing the region's importance for the country and downplaying the role of other regions. (According to Ivan Dziuba, the myth of Donbas as a sponsor of Ukraine was a local reflection of a broader all-Soviet myth about entire ethnic groups living off central government subsidies.)[24]

But the coal industry of independent Ukraine was neither profitable nor prestigious. The cost of coal mined in Donbas was so much higher than the price at which it was sold that the region received regular subsidies from the state budget, which peaked during the presidency of Viktor Yanukovych.[25] In 2012, the state budget received 21 billion hryvnias of revenue from the Donetsk and Luhansk regions but spent 44 billion hryvnias on the region's grants and subsidies.[26] Moreover, this financial support wasn't aimed at reforms and innovations and ended up in the pockets of the local elite. A report titled "The Real Price of Coal in the Context of the War in Donbas: A Human Rights Perspective," published by the Eastern Ukrainian Center for Civil Initiatives, revealed the following figures: in 2011, when violations of financial and budgetary discipline at the Makiivka Coal state enterprise caused damage valued at 1,823,500,000 hryvnias, Makiivka's municipal budget was only 877 million hryvnias.[27]

The number of mines and their employees was declining every year. In 1991, almost one million people were employed in the coal industry, but by 2013,

---

24 Ivan Dziuba, *Donets'ka rana Ukrainy: Istoryko-kul'turolohichni esei* [The Donetsk wound of Ukraine: Historical and cultural essays] (Kyiv: Natsional'naia akademiia nauk Ukrainy, 2015), 6.

25 Arseniy Yatsenyuk is credited with saying that it is cheaper to pay salaries to miners than to maintain unprofitable state-owned mines. (Source: Serhiy Holovn'ov, "Derzhavnyi vuhlevydobuvnyi sektor—'chorna dira' ukrainskoi ekonomiky" [The state coal mining sector is a "black hole" in the Ukrainian economy], Biznes Tsenzor, February 7, 2019, https://biz.censor.net/resonance/3110372/derjavnyi_vuglevidobuvniyi_sektor_chorna_dra_ukransko_ekonomki.)

26 "Dotatsiynyi Donbas. Chy spravdi rehion hoduie Ukrainu?" [Subsidized Donbas. Does the region really feed Ukraine?], *Ukrains'kyi tyzhden'*, February 28, 2013, https://tyzhden.ua/dotatsijnyj-donbas-chy-spravdi-rehion-hoduie-ukrainu/.

27 Denys Kazans'kyi, Anastasiia Nekrasova, et al., *Spravzhnia tsina vuhillia v umovakh viiny na Donbasi: pohliad kriz pryzmu prav liudyny* [The real price of coal in the context of the war in Donbas: A human rights perspective], (Kyiv: Art knyha, 2017), 33.

their number in the Donetsk region had fallen to 107,000.[28] This means that in 2013, in the Donetsk region, with its population of over four million people, miners accounted for only two percent (!) of all residents of the region.

In 1991, there were about 280 mines in Ukraine, particularly in Donbas and Western Ukraine (where the Lviv-Volyn coal basin is located). After 2014, there were only 35 mines in the government-controlled territory of Ukraine, and half of them were located in the Lviv-Volyn coal basin.[29] In 2020, the coal industry in the government-controlled territory of Ukraine employed only 35,000 people,[30] which takes this industry as far back as 1895, when it employed 32,000 people. It is safe to say that in 2014, mines and miners comprised only a part of the identity of the Donetsk and Luhansk regions, and often not a major one.

In independent Ukraine, the Soviet myth of Donbas was fueled and spread by the political elite. It successfully exploited such proletarian slogans as "No One Has Ever Brought Donbas to Its Knees"[31] (which in fact sounds like a propagandist post-truth, since the illegal exploitation of the labor, health, and lives of miners was the foundation of the mining industry), "Donbas Feeds the Whole of Ukraine," etc. During the 2004 presidential campaign, the local elite continued to appeal to Soviet myths[32] ("Pasha Angelina Is the Pride of Donbas!" or "Alexei Stakhanov Is a Prime Example of the Proletarian Character!").[33] In the 2010s, during the preparations for Euro 2012, the "Donbas" lexeme acquired a certain modern, even pro-Western gloss, becoming part of proper names such as the "Donbas Arena" or "Donbas Palace." Yet the toponym remained an artificial imperial construct.

The intuition of the above-mentioned researchers who wrote about "*Ukrainian* Donbas" didn't fail them: the myth of Donbas, which was created by the Soviet government and fostered in independent Ukraine, was established as anti-Ukrainian. That's why the descriptor "Ukrainian" preceding this toponym

28 O. Amosha, I. Buleiev, et al., *Promyslovist' Ukrainy 2014–2016: Nevykorystani mozhlyvosti, shliakhy vidnovlennia, modernizatsii ta suchasnoi rozbudovy: naukova dopovid'* [Industry of Ukraine in 2014–2016: Untapped opportunities, paths of recovery, modernization and modern development: A scientific report], Kyiv, 2017, https://iie.org.ua/wp-content/uploads/2017/04/Promislovist-Ukrayini_2017_16_05.pdf.

29 Serhiy Balan et al., *Otsinka efektyvnosti derzhavnykh vydatkiv na restrukturyzatsiiu vuhil'noi haluzi* [Evaluating the effectiveness of state spending on restructuring the coal industry], Dixi-Group NGO, 2020, 15.

30 Kazans'kyi, Nekrasova, et al., *Spravzhnia tsina vuhillia*, 33.

31 A line from a 1942 poem "Kliatva" [An oath] by Soviet miner and poet Pavlo Bezposhchadnyi.

32 Klinova, "Iak formuvalasia."

33 Evhen Sytnyk, "Chomu ya ne za YA., abo Pidkazky velykoho mista" [Why I don't support Ya., or the hints of a big city], *Dzerkalo tyzhnia*, November 12, 2004, https://zn.ua/ukr/internal/chomu_ya_ne_za_ya,_abo_pidkazky_velikogo_mista.html.

brings it back to a different coordinate system than the one it was intended to serve.

Donbas and the Ukrainian Language: A River Filled with Stones

In 2012, two years before the Russian aggression, the Rating polling organization conducted a survey on the language situation in Ukraine. In the survey, Donbas was defined as a separate macro-region. The survey results confirmed the well-known Russian-speaking character of the region: 83% of respondents described Russian as their main language of communication, and 10% said they used Russian and Ukrainian equally frequently. Only 7% of respondents chose Ukrainian as their main language of communication. These figures confirmed the image of Donbas as the most Russian-speaking region of the country.

Yet it shouldn't be assumed that this has always been the case. As historian Oleksandr Palii has aptly noted, the duration of "always" for people with interrupted historical memory is 50–70 years, or sometimes even less.[34] A closer look can reveal completely different details.

In its first and last census in 1897, the Russian Empire documented the predominant use of the Ukrainian language in some Ukrainian territories. In the Yekaterinoslav Governorate and Taganrog district of the Don Army region, which included the territories of the present-day Donetsk and Luhansk regions, 68.9% and 62% of the population respectively spoke Ukrainian.[35] Moreover, by the 1930s, the Ukrainian language was in an even stronger position in Russian-speaking communities, as the writer Borys Antonenko-Davydovych observed in 1929 of Yuzivka (as the city of Donetsk, named after Welsh engineer John Hughes, was then known): "Although practically all of the signs in Ukrainian contained errors, he senses with exhilaration that Ukrainization was progressing from below, from the mines and factories."[36] Until 1933, the Ukrainian-language magazine *Literary Donbas* was published

---

34 Oleksandr Palii, "Mistse pid sontsem, ne vkradene u susida" [A place under the sun not stolen from the neighbor], *Ukrains'ka pravda*, February 16, 2010, https://www.pravda.com.ua/columns/2010/02/16/4776323/.

35 The census recorded the divide in the population on the basis of their mother tongue. Source: *Etnichnyi sklad ukrainskykh hubernii (za danymy perepysu naselennia Rosiiskoi imperii 1897 r.)* [The ethnic structure of Ukrainian provinces (according to the 1897 Russian Empire census)], http://likbez.org.ua/ua/census-of-the-russian-empire-in-1897-ukrainian-province.html.

36 Kuromiya, *Freedom and Terror in the Donbas*, 197.

in Kostiantynivka.[37] The ideologist behind the Ukrainization policy of the 1920s, Mykola Skrypnyk, the second secretary of the Central Committee of the Communist Party of Ukraine, was born in the town of Yasynuvata in the Bakhmut district of the Yekaterinoslav Governorate.

The all-out attack on the Ukrainian language began with the Holodomor and the Great Terror. Hiroaki Kuromiya writes that the Soviet Terror was aimed at Ukrainization and those who advocated it: "Ukrainian teachers were fired and often arrested as 'class enemies.' In 1933 as many as 10 percent of teachers in the Ukrainian schools were branded as political enemies. In Donbas, the Ukrainian secondary schools were transformed wholesale to Russian-language instruction; technical schools used only Russian, treating Ukrainian as a foreign language. Many people involved in Ukrainization were repressed."[38] Moreover, "in the Donbas mines, workers were arrested for reading Ukrainian nationalist literature (by [Volodymyr] Vynnychenko and [Mykola] Kulish) and for hanging the late Skrypnyk's portrait in the dormitory. Some in Kadiivka were repressed for protesting against the use of Russian in meetings and for allegedly contending that 'Ukraine is under the [Russian] yoke.'"[39] Oleksandr Dovzhenko recalled in one of his 1942 diary entries: "There was a Taras Shevchenko institute in Voroshilovgrad [i.e. Luhansk], with Russian as the language of instruction, of course, and it didn't have a single Shevchenko book in its library. How original! There's nothing like it in the whole of Europe."[40] Intellectuals whose work chronologically belongs to the "Executed Renaissance" period were repressed in the 1930s, including Hryhoriy Bahliuk, editor of the Ukrainian-language magazines *Coal Face* and *Literary Donbas*, Sava Bozhko, and Lev Skrypnyk.

In 1932–1922, 79% of schoolchildren in the Donetsk region studied in Ukrainian; by 1945–1946, that figure had fallen to 66%.[41] By 1972, according to Oleksa Tykhyi's testimonies, in the towns of Kramatorsk, Druzhkivka, Kostiantynivka, Artemivsk, Horlivka, Zhdanov, and Donetsk, there were no Ukrainian schools at all,[42] and one could refuse to take the Ukrainian classes for

37 Marta Shokalo, "Sut' Donbasu—svoboda i teror" [The essence of Donbas is freedom and terror], BBC News Ukraine, December 23, 2009, https://www.bbc.com/ukrainian/ukraine/2009/12/091223_donbass_2_sp.
38 Kuromiya, *Freedom and Terror in the Donbas*, 197.
39 Ibid., 209.
40 Cited in Vira Ageyeva, *Behind the Scenes of the Empire: Essays on Cultural Relationships between Ukraine and Russia* (Stuttgart: Ibidem Press, 2023).
41 Palii, "Mistse pid sontsem."
42 Oleksa Tykhyi, *Rozdumy: Zbirnyk statei, dokumentiv, spohadiv* [Reflections: A collection of articles, documents, and memories] (Baltimore: Smoloskyp, 1982), 9–26.

"health reasons."[43] In 1989, only 8.7% of Ukrainian schools were still functioning in the Donetsk region, and even those were located only in villages. It is not surprising that "the relative number of Ukrainians who considered Ukrainian their native tongue decreased from census to census: 1959—87.6%, 1970—78.3%, 1979—71.6%, 1989—66.4%."[44]

Under these circumstances, it is particularly striking that the Ukrainian intellectual tradition continued in Donbas despite what Oleksa Tykhyi described as "intellectual genocide."[45] The fact that a number of dissidents from the Donetsk and Luhansk regions—representatives of the Ukrainian Sixtiers such as Ivan Svitlychnyi, Mykola Rudenko, Oleksa Tykhyi, Vasyl Stus, and Vasyl Holoborodko—emerged as Ukrainian writers under the most unfavorable conditions, further indicates that Donbas has Ukrainian roots and foregrounds how much greater the creative output of this region could have been had it not suffered from the "resource curse"—I use the term here to refer to the region's industrial importance in the eyes of the Russian authorities, which made it subject to not only colonial subjugation but also to particularly rigorous de-Ukrainization.

"Pockets" of Ukrainian were preserved only where the language was part of a professional specialization. In Soviet times, among the spaces that were Ukrainian-speaking or bilingual were the offices of the Union of Ukrainian Writers (every year, on Taras Shevchenko's birthday, the Ukrainian-speaking part of the Union went to the poet's monument to read his poetry), the editorial board of *Donbas* magazine (the magazine editor, Kost Mikheyiv, was Ukrainian-speaking and preferred Ukrainian texts), and the Departments of Ukrainian Philology, History of Ukraine, and Historiography and Source Studies at Donetsk National University.

The intellectuals of the Donetsk region—Volodymyr Biletskyi, Valentyna Tykha, Halyna Hordasevych, Anatoliy Zahnitko, and a number of their colleagues and associates—founded the Taras Shevchenko Ukrainian Language Society in Donetsk as soon as a window of opportunity opened in 1989—at that

---

43 "Although this was not the case everywhere"—Oksana Mikheieva, who went to school in Donetsk in 1977–1988, recalls how such permits were given only to children whose families moved frequently (for example, the children of military officers).

44 Nataliia Pashyna, *Etnomovnyi chynnyk politychnoi identychnosti v Donbasi* [The ethnolinguistic factor of political identity in Donbas], *Politychnyi menedzhment* 1 (2005): 29, https://ipiend. gov.ua/wp-content/uploads/2018/07/pashyna_etnomovnyi.pdf.

45 Oleksa Tykhyi, "Dumky pro ridnyi Donets'kyi krai" [Thoughts about my dear Donetsk region], *Holos Ukrainy*, 1972, https://olexa.org.ua/tvory/tvor01.htm.

time, there was still resistance to such initiatives, but it was already possible.[46] This situation continued until the Russian invasion in 2014: the movements and communities of the first wave (the 1990s) and the second (the 2000s and early 2010s) existed under conditions of absolute hostility and resistance from the authorities. Back in 1989, Gennady Yerkhov, the secretary of the regional committee of the Communist Party of Ukraine, claimed in Russian: "*On my watch as the secretary of the regional committee, there will never be a Ukrainian language society here in Donetsk region,*" while in 1990, Mykhailo Hirschman, the head of the commission of public education at Donetsk City Council, stated that "the opening of a school with Ukrainian as the language of instruction is an act of violence against the people."[47] This resistance continued until 2014, when the local Euromaidan protests were dispersed by armed mobs of men known as *titushky*.

At the same time, there was public demand for the Ukrainian language in the early 1990s. Stanislav Fedorchuk, a historian from Donetsk, recalls the story of his father, who was a member of Donetsk City Council: "In the 1990s election, [my father] defeated the party secretary of the Donetsk Metallurgical Plant. During the debates, voters asked whether the candidates knew Ukrainian. [...] Well, that party secretary was originally from the Urals and couldn't put two words together in Ukrainian. When my father started speaking Ukrainian, the people who'd come to the debates started applauding him. And he won the elections."[48] Leonid Hromovyi, a dissident who founded the first Ukrainian-medium secondary school in Donetsk, also felt the demand for Ukrainian. According to Hromovyi, the school's founding was supported by members of the Supreme Soviet of the USSR as well as Yevgeny Yevtushenko and Andrei Sakharov, two

---

46 The extent of the tolerance toward the Ukrainian language is evident in the experience of Mykola Melnychenko, lecturer at the Department of Mathematics at Donetsk State University: in 1968, he was only into the forty-fifth minute of his lecture delivered in Ukrainian when he was reported to the dean; in 1989, he managed to deliver three lectures in Ukrainian, and in 1993, he lectured in Ukrainian for several weeks. Source: Volodymyr Bilets'kyi et al., *My ydemo!: narysy z istorii Donets'koho oblasnoho tovarystva ukrains'koi movy im. T. H. Shevchenka—pershoi masovoi natsional'no-demokratychnoi hromads'koi orhanizatsii Donechchyny* [We're coming!: Essays on the history of the Taras Shevchenko Donetsk regional society of the Ukrainian language, the first major national democratic public organization in Donetsk region] (Donets'k: Skhid, 1998), 135.

47 Ibid., 11 and 108.

48 Andrii Olenin, "Donbas: Nevtrachene pokolinnia" [Donbas: the unlost generation], part 1, LB.ua, August 12, 2021, https://lb.ua/society/2021/08/12/491303_donbas_nevtrachene_pokolinnya_ch1.html. It's important to note that in the March 1990 elections to Donetsk City Council, independent candidates secured a majority, while representatives of the Communist Party were in a minority.

Soviet dissidents, and became the first school in the USSR to recruit both teachers and students on a competitive basis. Among the boys, there were about 18–22 applicants per place, and among the girls, there were up to 28 applicants per place.[49] Although this level of interest was presumably due as much to the quality of the teaching as the fact that Ukrainian was the language of instruction, it also reveals that parents of Donetsk children had nothing against their children being educated in Ukrainian. The school became the place where the first group of the Ukrainian scouting organization Plast in Donetsk and other pro-Ukrainian public organizations began to take root.

Yet, as Ukraine became independent, Donbas wasn't given a chance at Ukrainization. More schools were offering Ukrainian as the language of instruction (though often these were not entire schools, but Ukrainian-speaking classes that existed alongside Russian-speaking ones): in 1991, only 3% of schoolchildren in the Donetsk region studied in Ukrainian, but by 2012 their number had increased to 48.4%.[50] Yet the problem was that outside of school, Ukrainian remained marginalized and unneeded. Moreover, as journalist and columnist Maksym Vikhrov has observed, after the Orange Revolution, "it became much more difficult to engage in educational work: any campaign aimed at popularizing Ukrainian language and culture was perceived as a political invasion of 'the Orange.' And yet the Ukrainian language wasn't rejected entirely: Luhansk cinemas showed Ukrainian-language films, and concerts by Okean Elzy, a popular Ukrainian rock band, would sell out. This didn't change the attitude toward the Ukrainian language: it was still considered optional, and Ukrainian was seen as a whim of crazy nationalists from Lviv."[51]

The "pockets" of Ukrainization, particularly in education, were being slowly destroyed: in the early 2000s, Leonid Hromovyi was fired. In 2004, the last Ukrainian-medium secondary school in Donetsk was closed. In 2005, out of 990 periodicals published in the Donetsk region, only 19 (or 2%) were in

---

49 Stanislav Fedorchuk, "Osvita ne mozhe buty pidporiadkovana mistsevii vladi: Interv'iu z Leonidom Hromovym" [Education cannot be controlled by the local government: An interview with Leonid Hromov], *Den'*, March 18, 2009, https://rozmova.wordpress.com/2018/11/18/leonid-hromovyi/.

50 Pavel Ostrovskii, "V Donetskoi oblasti ezhegodno rastet kolichestvo shkol'nikov, kotorye vybiraiut ukrainskii iazyk (infografika)" [In Donetsk region, the number of schoolchildren who choose to study the Ukrainian language is growing every year (infographics)], *Novyny Donbasu*, February 21, 2012, https://novosti.dn.ua/ru/article/3882-vdoneckoy-oblasty-ezhegodno-rastet-kolychestvo-shkolnykov-kotorye-vybyrayut-ukraynskyy-yazyk-ynfografyka.

51 Maksym Vikhrov, "Chy mozhlyva ukrainizatsiia? Mirkuiuchy pro keis Donbasu" [Is Ukrainization possible? Considering the case of Donbas], *Krytyka* 1–2 (2018): 243–244.

Ukrainian, and they had tiny print runs.[52] In the 2000s, there were hardly any Ukrainian-language spaces left in Donetsk. The only public spaces where one could hear Ukrainian were cafés and restaurants—McDonald's, Puzata Khata, and Lviv Handmade Chocolate—where the service was in Ukrainian.[53]

A particularly shocking illustration of the Ukrainian language situation in the Donetsk region in independent Ukraine is that the number of citizens who considered Ukrainian their mother tongue has decreased since Ukraine became independent. In 1989, 66.4% of local Ukrainians considered Ukrainian their native tongue, but in 2001, only 41.2% of them did. In the Luhansk region the same year, the number of people who considered Ukrainian their native tongue was slightly higher, at 50.4%.[54]

There's another linguistic phenomenon worth mentioning that's often over-looked: the split into the Ukrainian and Russian languages, and accordingly, into Ukrainian speakers and Russian speakers, is not as clear-cut as it might seem when looking at tables of statistics. According to Volodymyr Rafeyenko, a writer from Donetsk and Russian studies scholar, "[t]here has never been an abyss between these two languages, because the Russian language spoken in Donbas is very different from the Russian spoken in Russia, while the Ukrainian language, under the influence of Russian, has been transforming into its eastern variant." I heard similar arguments from my interviewees from the East.

"At our market, people speak only Ukrainian. Well, a version of Ukrainian, *surzhyk*;" "In Donbas, there's no pure Russian language. There's *surzhyk*—a word in Ukrainian followed by a word in Russian." I have heard both opinions.

And finally, we shouldn't equate languages with political views. As Andriy Portnov aptly puts it, in the 1990s and the 2000s in Ukraine, "people who were Russian speakers didn't necessarily have pro-Russian political views"[55] (and Ukrainian speakers, I should add, weren't necessarily patriots of Ukraine). The

---

52 Bilets'kyi, *Skhid Ukrainy v intehratyvnykh protsesakh suchasnoho derzhavotvorennia* [Eastern Ukraine in the integrative processes of modern state formation] (Donets'k: Skhid, 2005), 15, 16.

53 In his book *In Isolation*, Stanislav Aseyev mentions the Lviv Handmade Chocolate café as an island of Ukrainian identity in already occupied Donetsk: "While people from Kyiv and Lviv were outraged by the fact that Lviv Handmade Chocolate was still operating in Donetsk, the author would visit it from time to time—for him, those were moments of utter delight and imaginary connection with the rest of Ukraine." Stanislav Aseyev, *In Isolation: Dispatches from Occupied Donbas*, trans. Lidia Wolanskyj (Cambridge: Harvard University Press, 2022), 12.

54 See the results of 2001 Ukrainian census at "Vseukrains'kyi perepys naselennia 2001," Derzhavnyi komitet statystyky Ukrainy, http://2001.ukrcensus.gov.ua/. Let's not forget that Ukrainians constituted only about 60% of the population of the Donetsk and Luhansk regions, while Russians made up almost 40% of the population (see Table 1).

55 Portnov, "Svoboda ta vybir na Donbasi."

Donetsk region of the 1990s and 2000s lacked many cultural and educational processes that were slowly unfolding in Lviv and Kyiv, it remained in the orbit of Russian television and Soviet mythologies, yet it definitely wasn't anti-Ukrainian.

The Myth of Separatism: "The Autonomy We didn't Want"

"The Autonomy We Didn't Want"[56] is the title of an article by Kostiantyn Reutskyi, a human rights activist from Luhansk. In the article, the author consistently debunks the myth of the distinctive nature of Donbas—starting with the fact that "Donbas" as a toponym is used to describe very heterogeneous territories, and ending with an analysis of the linguistic, industrial, and religious characteristics of the region. Kostiantyn Reutskyi compares the characteristics of Donbas with those of other Ukrainian regions and proves that they are not unique. For instance, the high proportion of Russians in the population of Donbas (see Table 1) is often cited as an argument, yet the pre-war figures in the Kharkiv, Odesa, and Zaporizhzhia regions were similar.

Table 1. The ethnic composition of the Donetsk and Luhansk regions, according to the 2001 census.[57]

	Donetsk Region (%)	Luhansk Region (%)
Ukrainians	56.9	58.0
Russians	38.2	39.0

In the 1991 referendum, the vast majority of the population of the Donetsk and Luhansk regions voted in favor of Ukraine's independence (83.9% of residents of the Donetsk region (out of 76.7% who participated in the referendum) and 83.86% of residents of the Luhansk region (out of 80.7% of voters).

In 1994, 1999, and 2004, Yaroslav Hrytsak, Andriy Portnov, and Viktor Susaka conducted research that came out under the title "Lviv—Donetsk. Social Identities in Modern Ukraine."[58] Despite the distinct national identity of

---

56 Kostiantyn Reuts'kyi, "Donbas. Avtonomiia, iakoi my ne prahnuly" [Donbas: The autonomy we didn't want], *Ukrains'ka pravda*, February 8, 2021, https://www.pravda.com.ua/columns/2021/02/8/7282612/.

57 See the data of the census at "Publikatsii," "Vseukrains'kyi perepys naselennia 2001," Derzhavnyi komitet statystyky Ukrainy, http://2001.ukrcensus.gov.ua/publications/#p4.

58 Iaroslav Hrytsak, Andrii Portnov, et al., "Lviv—Donets'k. Sotsial'ni identychnosti u suchasnii Ukraini" [Lviv—Donetsk. Social identities in modern Ukraine], *Krytyka* 7 (2007): 47–122.

Donetsk, which was much more pronounced than in Lviv, it's also worth noting that 74.2% of respondents believed that their region had a common future with the rest of Ukraine, and for 73% of respondents, the integrity of Ukraine was more important than the needs of individual regions.

Finally, and I quote Reutskyi here, until 2014, there were "no serious and widely (or professionally) discussed publications putting forward arguments supporting the autonomy of the region or its secession from Ukraine. There were no protests, demonstrations, or any other mass campaigns that called for the autonomy of the Ukrainian East. There were no 'heroes of the fight for the autonomy of Donbas' being persecuted by the special services or imprisoned."

Of course, there were people in the region who didn't share pro-Ukrainian views (such people can be found in any region of Ukraine). And yet they didn't comprise the majority of the region. In 2014, there were residents of Donbas who did support unification with Russia and were proponents of any form of separatism, but they comprised the minority. According to surveys conducted by the Rating Group and the Ilko Kucheriv Democratic Initiatives Foundation, no more than a third of the population shared this sentiment.[59]

Yevhen Sereda, a journalist with the news outlet *Ukrainska pravda*, tried to find out where the myth of separatism in Donbas originated, and concluded that media coverage played a significant role: for the rest of Ukraine, the image of an aggressive and loud minority formed an association with the entire region.[60]

***

Once I learned all this, I couldn't quite bring myself to call the Donetsk and Luhansk regions "Donbas."

---

59 Evhen Sereda, "Piat' rokiv 'rosiiskii vesni'. Iak sformuvavsia mif pro separatyzm na Donbasi" [The Fifth anniversary of the "Russian spring." How the myth of separatism in Donbas was formed], *Ukrains'ka pravda*, April 12, 2019, https://www.pravda.com.ua/articles/2019/04/12/7211983/.

60 Ibid. The fact that the regional political elite and Russia had been seriously preparing for the 2014 scenario for a long time is another issue. We shouldn't forget the congress of "party members of all levels" (mostly the Party of Regions) on November 28, 2004, five days after the second round of the presidential elections. The "delegates" put forward the idea of a separate "South-Eastern Ukrainian Autonomous Republic" that would include eight eastern and southern regions of Ukraine and Crimea, with the center in Kharkiv. Moscow Mayor Yuri Luzhkov was among the guests at the congress. In a 2006 interview, Aleksandr Dugin, an ideologist of the "Russian World," in response to a question about what Russia would do if Ukraine joined NATO, used very precise language: "We will withdraw economic support from Ukraine. First of all, we will cut off its gas. Additionally, in this situation, Moscow, diplomatically speaking, *will cease to contain separatist sentiments in Crimea and Eastern Ukraine* [italics mine—K.Z.]," *Gorod*, September 15, 2006.

In some instances, however, I still use this toponym in my book only as the most recognizable version of a name that encompasses both the Donetsk and Luhansk regions. But often it's simply inappropriate, and instead, I'll use the name of the place where the events actually took place: Donetsk or Luhansk region. As for "Donbas" as a toponym, only time will tell whether it will continue to be used (and if so, in what sense), or whether it will be thrown out like monuments to Lenin.

***

Does the region have a special identity?

From the point of view of sociology, it is wrong to deny the existence of a regional identity—after all, Donbas and Ukraine are not the only places where people can identify with their regional homeland and feel attached to it. Yet regional identity is not the same as an artificially created myth, and in the case of the bizarre "Donbas identity" (I believe that this phrase can only be used as a joke, and it's better not to use it at all, because by verbalizing it we legitimize it), any attempts to reveal it only reinforce the myth rather than explain anything. In one of his interviews, Vasyl Holoborodko complained, "They always tried to regionalize me: you're from Donbas, you're from the East. Whereas I've never considered myself a Donbas author. The critic Leonid Kovalenko always asked me why I didn't have poems about Donbas, about the mine, didn't I work there, after all? But I work in Ukrainian and I don't care if I live in Rostov, Luhansk, or Rio de Janeiro. *I live in the Ukrainian language* [italics mine—K.Z.]."[61]

Even in our conversations with people from the region, I sometimes encountered a kind of self-blame or self-criticism, coupled with apologies that were supposed to emphasize the same stereotypical identity but, in fact, only denied it once again, because what they think makes them distinct is just as common elsewhere. For instance, one professor noted with sorrow during our conversation that in the 1990s, people in Donetsk celebrated the New Year twice: an hour earlier than the rest of Ukraine, on Moscow time, and then again on Kyiv time. Trying to adhere to the rules of interviewing and not to express my own opinions, I didn't dare to tell him that in my childhood in Kyiv in the 1990s, I saw some people do the same.

---

61 Halyna Tanai, "Holoborod'ko: Putin—postmodernist, shcho ne mae niiakykh tsinnostei" [Holoborodko: Putin is a postmodernist who has no values], *Chytomo*, December 2, 2014, https://archive.chytomo.com/interview/goloborodko-putin-spravzhnij-postmodernist-shho-ne-maye-niyakix-cinnostej.

Again, in one of the villages in the Donetsk region, a local activist complained to me: "Can you imagine, children from Ukrainian-speaking families study in Ukrainian, but during the breaks between classes, they speak Russian?" Yes, I can definitely imagine that, because I've witnessed the same thing in my children's school in Kyiv.

***

A Ukrainian Donbas, in its Soviet or post-Soviet sense, didn't exist as such. Yet Ukrainian Donetsk and Luhansk regions did and do exist, and the decision to ignore them, to paraphrase Ivan Dziuba, can only be explained by laziness of thought or political bias.[62] Since Ukraine became independent, they have been best manifest in relatively small communities—small enough to remain invisible to the eyes of official statistics, yet numerous enough for those who belonged to them to find like-minded people.

This book is about the communities whose existence has been denied by the Donbas myth. It's about cultural spaces, student communities, Ukrainian villages, and the diversity of religious centers. It's about people who wanted to live not in a dictatorship but in a free, modern, democratic Ukraine.

These communities have been the voices of the new, non-post-Soviet Donetsk and Luhansk regions embedded in the nationwide Ukrainian context. They have been the awakening of the dormant (oppressed, exterminated, tortured) Ukrainian identity.

The aim of this book is to bring to the fore at least a fragment of the history of these communities.

---

62 See Dziuba, *Donets'ka rana Ukrainy*, 18. "Only laziness of thought or political bias can explain, on the one hand, the endless attempts to deny or diminish the presence of the Ukrainian ethnic element in this territory since the sixteenth century, and, on the other hand, the ignoring of the scale of migration flows in the nineteenth and twentieth centuries, and the state's voluntaristic supply of the ambitious industrial development in the Ukrainian SSR with labor force, which resulted in the accumulation of ethnic and cultural problems and contradictions."

Chapter 2

The Story of Poshtovkh

"We Only Needed Ten More Years"

In January 2017, I recorded an interview with Serhiy Stukanov at the Kupidon literary café. Serhiy had just moved to Kyiv from Lviv, where he had initially relocated after fleeing the occupied territories. We had met for the first time at Hromadske Radio, where he worked as a presenter.

Until 2014, Serhiy and his friends had been among the drivers of the "Ukrainian Renaissance" in the Donetsk region. In 2011, he enrolled as a history student at what is now Vasyl Stus Donetsk National University, but at the time was known simply as Donetsk National University (DonNU).

The universities of Donetsk and Luhansk became centers of national revival. Volodymyr Biletskyi, a doctor of engineering and professor at Donetsk National Technical University, was the founder and editor of *Skhid* magazine and the newspaper *Skhidnyi chasopys*, actively integrating Donbas into the broader Ukrainian context through his research and his publications. Volodymyr Semystiaha, a senior lecturer at the Department of Ukrainian History at Luhansk State University, is the head of the Luhansk branch of the Taras Shevchenko Prosvita Society.

It was the history departments of universities in both Donetsk and Luhansk that nurtured the entire community, and the war and forced displacement after 2014 only further highlighted the plethora of Ukrainian intellectuals of a European level. Oksana Mikheieva, Olena Stiazhkina, Ihor Todorov, Stanislav Fedorchuk, and many others moved to Kyiv, Lviv, Uzhhorod, and other cities, becoming spokespeople, or "alternative voices," for the region. Yet even in their "home" community, they could and did influence the perception of history: In1989, the faculty and students of Donetsk National University began unauthorized excavations at the Rutchenkovo Field (in the then Kirovskyi district of Donetsk) and proved that it was victims of Stalinist repressions that were buried in the local mass graves, and not prisoners of war shot by Nazis, as previously thought.[1]

What made the History Department so different? Was it the discipline itself—history—that shaped a certain personality type, marked by critical thinking and good citizenship? Or was it the other way round—was it the History Department that attracted socially conscious young people? Ihor Todorov, a former professor at Donetsk National University, believes that "the spirit of the Department involved a kind of freedom," and that is why Todorov has taught solely in Ukrainian since 2000.[2] He recalled how his international relations students (Todorov eventually began teaching in this program) were happy to speak Ukrainian during their seminars, explaining: "We want to build a career in this country, and where else can we practice Ukrainian in Donetsk if not at the university?" The only member of the faculty who did not teach in Ukrainian was the head of the Department of International Relations, who was from the Urals.[3] Serhiy Stukanov recalled preparing for the classes in Russian, but the lecturers demanded answers in Ukrainian.

Yet, freedom at the department meant freedom for everyone—people of different, sometimes opposing views gravitated toward it and came together there, as is generally common for Donbas. The pro-Ukrainian positions held by Todorov, Matushchak, Stukanov, and others were not universally shared: Serhiy Baryshnikov, for example, a lecturer at the Department of Political Science, made no secret of his anti-Ukrainian stance in class,[4] and Pavlo Hubarev, a

1 Oksana Mikheieva talks about participating in the excavations in Zoya Ryazantseva's program *Storinky istorii* [Pages of history] (Donetsk Regional State TV and Radio Company), 2007, https://www.youtube.com/watch?v=0igfqI2EKlA. More about the Rutchenkovo Field can be found here: "Rutchenkovo pole—rasstrel'nyi poligon NKVD v Donetske" [Rutchenkovo field—The shooting polygon of the NKVD in Donetsk], Antisovetskii blog, Livejournal, October 4, 2017, https://antisovetsky.livejournal.com/10325.html.
2 Interview with Ihor Todorov, February 2, 2021.
3 Ibid.
4 Vitaliy Ovcharenko recalled that during a lecture on world history, the lecturer Baryshnikov asked in Russian: "Dear boys and girls, who among you will grieve if the state of Ukraine

graduate of the History Department, became an active member of the "DPR." "We were too liberal," Todorov concluded sorrowfully, looking back on the past.

***

In October 2006, a dark-haired boy approached third-year student Serhiy Zlyvko at a student conference on European integration.

"Hey, I see that you're interested in Ukraine. We're launching a pro-Ukrainian patriotic organization. You're welcome to join us."

That's how Serhiy met Yuriy Matushchak and became a member of Poshtovkh, or "Impulse," an iconic organization in Donetsk in the early 2000s. It was founded on October 31, 2006 by eighteen young men and women, mostly students at the History and Languages and Literature Departments of Donetsk National University, and a few students from the Donetsk National University of Artificial Intelligence and Donetsk National Technical University. They realized that the key to the hearts and minds of the local population lay in understanding history. "We thought that if we educated people about the history of the region and explained that Ukrainian culture was not inferior to Russian culture, then we would be contributing to the integration of this region into the general cultural landscape of Ukraine," Stukanov recalled.

Ultimately, Poshtovkh became a vivid chapter in the story of the Ukrainian national revival in Donbas in the second half of the 2000s, and Yuriy (or Yura, Yurko, as his friends called him) Matushchak became the heart of the organization, embodying the new generation of the Ukrainian movement in the region. The scale of Poshtovkh's achievements is even more impressive considering that its members and supporters were students and young people who had neither financial nor administrative resources, only a bunch of interesting ideas and a desire to create change. In just a few short years (2007–2009), they contributed to national revival in the region more than anyone before them in the years since Ukraine's independence.

The students held their first demonstration on Unity Day: On January 22, 2007, they gathered at the Taras Shevchenko monument in Donetsk holding a placard that read: "Greetings to Donetsk residents from Poshtovkh." The campaigns that followed grew increasingly larger in scale: in 2008 and 2009,

---

ceases to exist?" Source: "Diialnist' 'Poshtovkhu'—velykyi arhument za ukrains'kyi Donbas,— aktyvisty" ["Poshtovkh's work is a major argument for Ukrainian Donbas," activists say], *Hromads'ke radio*, October 28, 2016, https://hromadske.radio/podcasts/kyiv-donbas/diyalnist-poshtovhu-velykyy-argument-za-ukrayinskyy-donbas-aktyvisty.

Poshtovkh held a Vertep[5] Festival (the first one was held outside near Lenin Square, and the second one in the city's Yunist Youth Palace), co-organized an exhibition about the Ukrainian Insurgent Army called "UPA: History of the Unconquered" in Donetsk, and held a Holodomor commemoration event. The organization was among the originators of the campaign to have Donetsk National University named after Vasyl Stus, and the students also organized poetry slams.

How did these young people manage to accomplish all this without connections or money, and in opposition to the local authorities, who quickly realized that Poshtovkh's work was in conflict with their ideology and program? Leonid Samofalov, a close friend of Yuriy Matushchak's and co-founder of Poshtovkh, recalled: "Poshtovkh taught me that nothing was impossible". The students simply had the courage to knock on every door. When, in 2008, the city authorities did not want to grant permission to hold the Vertep Festival in Donetsk's main square, Poshtovkh was helped by an MP from the Our Ukraine—People's Self-Defense party after the young men and women went to his office during visiting hours. On another occasion, it was a stroke of luck and their willingness to take risks that proved decisive: While traveling through western Ukraine, Poshtovkh members left an invitation to the Vertep Festival under the door of the Ivano-Frankivsk State Administration on their last night in the city, right before getting their train back. Of all the invitations they sent out to various regional administrations, it was this one that got results: A *vertep* from Ivano-Frankivsk came to Donetsk for the festival.

Poshtovkh also initiated the exhibition "UPA: History of the Unconquered," which was held in Donetsk. The exhibition was organized by the Institute of National Memory with the support of the Security Service of Ukraine (SBU). It toured many Ukrainian cities. However, the reason why the exhibition could be held in Donetsk was that Yuriy Matushchak wrote a letter to Volodymyr Viatrovych, then the Research Advisor to the Head of the SBU. The exhibition was held in the Nadia Krupska Donetsk Regional Universal Library,[6] and Poshtovkh members gave tours to visitors.[7]

---

5   A portable puppet theater, originally for presenting the Christmas story and other mystery plays (translator's note).

6   "V Donets'ku rozpovidaly pro UPA" [Stories about the UPA were told in Donetsk], Ukrains'ka povstans'ka armiia. Istoriia neskorenykh, February 19, 2008, http://upa.in.ua/book/?p=41.

7   It is worth noting that in Luhansk the opening of the exhibition was disrupted by followers of the Party of Regions and the Communist Party, who blocked the entrance to the building and fought with Svoboda Party sympathizers who were attempting to visit the exhibition. See Vikhrov, *Dykyi skhid*, 268–269.

Another campaign intended to foster national revival in Donetsk was a commemoration of the Holodomor victims entitled "33 Minutes." Poshtovkh members gathered in front of district administrations in Donetsk and, for thirty-three minutes, read aloud the names of the locals who perished during the Holodomor. There were usually many names still to be read on the list after the time was over. "I don't know what kind of impression it made on those who listened to us, but for me, it was mind-blowing," Marta Chorna, a member of Poshtovkh, recalled.

Poshtovkh also published its own newspaper, *Poshtovkh+* (the name of the newspaper featured a symbolic trident instead of the Ukrainian letter "ш"). The newspaper was published only twice, but the process of creating it was highly professional: It was officially registered as a print media outlet, had an editorial board (comprising Yuriy Matushchak, Marta Chorna, Leonid Samofalov, and Serhiy Zlyvko) and an editor (Serhiy Stukanov, who went by the pseudonym Serhiy Lozanovskyi in the second issue), and over ten people contributed to this eight-page publication. Along with articles authored by writers just starting out—students in particular—*Poshtovkh+* featured such luminaries as the writer Yuriy Andrukhovych and the historian Stanislav Kulchytskyi. The newspaper's founders financed the publication out of their own pockets, partly from the modest membership fees, but mostly with funds provided by Matushchak and Samofalov.

Poshtovkh's work was fueled by two related circumstances. First, the organization was founded and became active during the presidency of Viktor Yushchenko. His policy of restoring historical memory was encouraging for Poshtovkh, as its members felt that their work was in line with the nationwide movement toward linguistic and cultural revival. Secondly, given the hostile attitude of the city authorities, the organization found a political ally in the Regional State Administration, whose head was appointed by the president. This translated into a level of support for the organization: for example, it was the Regional State Administration that provided security (!) for the exhibition "UPA: History of the Unconquered" at Donetsk library with police on duty. In 2009, Lilia Zolkina, head of the Regional State Administration's Department of Family and Young People, helped Poshtovkh to organize the Vertep Festival at the Yunist Donetsk Youth Palace.

The university administration and Donetsk political circles, however, were tolerant rather than approving of the organization's work, and sometimes even obstructed its efforts. In addition to the already mentioned difficulties obtaining permission to hold the Vertep Festival, the organization also faced opposition from the university administration. In 2009, Tetiana Marmazova, the vice president for academic affairs, opposed the idea that participants in the Second Vertep Festival be accommodated in a student dormitory (the matter was eventually settled with the help of friends of Poshtovkh's from the Faculty of Law). But there was no open confrontation between the organization and its opponents as long as an ideological clash which involved choosing a single identity for the university could be avoided. For Donetsk National University, such an ideological clash occurred during the campaign to have the university named after Vasyl Stus.

The fight for Vasyl Stus

From the perspective of today, it may be difficult to understand why the figure of Vasyl Stus was viewed so ambiguously in Donetsk. Stus, a dissident poet, translator, literary critic, and journalist, was a graduate of Donetsk National University (which even had a plaque commemorating him in its Philology Department) who was awarded the title of Hero of Ukraine in 2005 and whose works had been on the school curriculum in Ukrainian literature since the 1990s. Those who campaigned for Donetsk National University to be named after Vasyl Stus are convinced that the Donetsk political elite saw the campaign as "marking territory" that they considered their own and where there was no place for Ukrainians who fought against the Soviet regime.[8] The attitude toward Vasyl Stus became a litmus test that indicated the fault lines in the Donetsk community of the time: in one paradigm, that of independent Ukraine, Stus was a hero, while in the other, the post-Soviet one, he remained an "enemy of the people."

The idea of renaming a location—and not just the university—after Vasyl Stus had long been discussed. Such proposals were first voiced in the 1990s with regard to one of Donetsk's central streets, Postysheva Street, which had been named after one of the orchestrators of the Holodomor in Ukraine. Representatives of the "older generation" of pro-Ukrainian NGOs repeatedly advocated for Postysheva Street to be renamed after Vasyl Stus. Yet the city authorities rejected these requests, citing bureaucratic and financial constraints.

At the end of 2008, when the seventieth anniversary of Stus's birth was commemorated, members of Poshtovkh thought it was a good opportunity to launch a project to rename the university. Representatives of the Public Initiative of the

---

8   Vasyl Stus (1938 - 1985) died in a Soviet forced prison camp for political prisoners, five
    years into serving 15-year sentence and just six years before the collapse of the Soviet Union
    (author's note).

Donetsk Region for the Restoration of Historical Memory and Poshtovkh, led by Stanislav Fedorchuk and Yuriy Matushchak respectively, wrote an appeal on behalf of former and current students arguing that Donetsk National University should be renamed after Vasyl Stus.

At the same time, the initiative group was collecting signatures from students and faculty members of the university, which evolved into a major appeal by Ukrainian intellectuals to the Minister of Education and Science that was published in the newspapers *Den* and *Insha literatura*. The list of signatories included people from beyond Donetsk: Today, approximately 1,500 signatures from all over Ukraine and abroad can be found in the *Den* archives.[9] Ultimately, the initiative to rename the regional university reached the national level, with then President Viktor Yushchenko, Minister of Education and Science Ivan Vakarchuk, and members of the Verkhovna Rada (Parliament) all speaking out on the issue. Yushchenko supported the initiative, requesting that Vakarchuk and the head of the Donetsk regional state administration, Volodymyr Lohvynenko, consider the students' demands.[10] Instead, Olena Bondarenko, an MP from the Party of Regions (also a graduate of the university's History Department) who came to Donetsk on behalf of a commission authorized to assess the pros and cons of the student initiative, suggested naming the university after Volodymyr Degtyaryov, the first secretary of the Donetsk regional committee of the Communist Party in 1963–1976. The discussion caught the attention of other political parties: MPs from the Party of Regions and the Yulia Tymoshenko Bloc supported the university being renamed in honor of Degtyaryov, while the parliamentary group For Ukraine! proposed that the Verkhovna Rada consider a resolution renaming Donetsk National University after Vasyl Stus.[11]

As the campaigners recalled, a "life-and-death battle" broke out in Donetsk. The pro-Russian camp held roundtables and conferences on the issue. The vice president for academic affairs, Tetiana Marmazova—who was married to Ruslan Marmazov, press secretary of the Shakhtar soccer club—organized a campaign against renaming the university after Vasyl Stus. The organizers, however, did not want to be accused of holding anti-Ukrainian views—statehood was still the common denominator shared by even those who opposed the idea of renaming

9 "Donets'komu universitetovi—im'ia Stusa" [Stus's Name for Donetsk University], *Den'*, https://day.kyiv.ua/uk/doneckomu-universitetovi-imya-stusa.

10 Olha Reshetylova, "Prezy dent pidtry mav initsiatyvu studentiv" [President supports students' initiative], *Den'*, February 10, 2009, https://day.kyiv.ua/uk/article/panorama-dnya/prezident-pidtrimav-iniciativu-studentiv.

11 For more information on the initiative to rename Donetsk National University in honor of Vasyl Stus, see "Istoriia pytannia" [History of the issue], a special page on the Vasyl Stus Donetsk National University website, http://stus2016.donnu.edu.ua/home/istoria-pitanna.

the university after Stus—and the campaign was called "For the National," referring to the preservation of the university's current name. Blue and yellow rib-
bons were distributed at the event as a testament to the pro-Ukrainian views of
the participants. Students were told that naming the university after Stus would
result in the institution's accreditation being revoked, which was a blatant lie.

Not only did the letter from the ministry not help to resolve the issue in favor
of the students, it actually had the opposite effect: The university administration interpreted the request from the "center" as pressure and saw Poshtovkh
as agents of the "Orange" government and "Banderite nationalists."[12] The local
authorities refused to believe that such an initiative could have come from the
grassroots in a city like Donetsk and considered it a "Banderite" encroachment
on their territory.

The "For Stus" campaign even prompted the release of a Russian-language
publication entitled *Ukrainian Nationalism and Donbas: A Historical Perspective*,
in which the authors condemned the "historiography of 'Ukrainocentrism.'" Its
editorial board included Ihor Zhytnytskyi, a member of the regional administration from the Communist Party, and Donetsk National University professors
Tetiana Marmazova, Oleksandr Dynhes, and Serhiy Baryshnikov.

Eventually, at a meeting of the Donetsk National University faculty, 61 of
the 63 attendees voted against renaming the university. Poshtovkh was publicly
condemned from the rostrum, and a campaign was launched to vilify the organization among first-year students.[13] Talking about being a member of Postovkh
became dangerous, and students who took part in its events were publicly
shamed. It is worth noting that the campaign to rename the university revealed
that in Donetsk in the early 2000s, *what* was discussed mattered more than the
language used in the discussion: even a Ukrainian-language teacher (!) joined
the attacks on those in favor of the renaming. The dean himself attended the
defense of Leonid Samofalov's thesis and gave him a C, even though Leonid
had won student history competitions and was one of the brightest students
in his cohort (though later the faculty backtracked on the unfair grading and
organized a retake for him). Stukanov recalled that he felt as if he had suddenly

---

12 It is worth noting that while the word "Banderite" was synonymous with "criminal" for Party of
Regions and Communist Party supporters, not all representatives of the regime were aware of
what it actually meant. Legend has it that once, when the police were raiding student dormitories in search of nationalists, they asked if there were any supporters of Ostap Bender among the
students (apparently confusing Stepan Bandera with the character from Ilf and Petrov's novels).

13 Olena Panych, "Iak Donets'kyi universytet ne dav prysvoity sobi im'ia Vasylia Stusa" [How
Donetsk university refused to be named after Vasyl Stus], *Istorychna pravda*, August 16, 2014,
https://www.istpravda.com.ua/blogs/53ee893ab679a/.

found himself almost back in the Stalinist era, which he and his classmates had just been discussing and examining in their history classes.[14]

After 2009, Poshtovkh's work on various campaigns slowed down, although it did not disappear completely. Some of its most active members, such as Yuriy Matushchak, graduated from the university, and those who might have replenished the organization's ranks were threatened. For a while, Poshtovkh ran cultural and political campaigns as an autonomous (not university-affiliated) organization. For example, they held art competitions for children and literary evenings, and in 2012, they organized a campaign in support of the artist Petro Antyp, who was running for parliamentary elections in Horlivka. (Poshtovkh members delivered leaflets, campaigned, and served in the commission at every polling station in the city.)

Some Poshtovkh members stayed in Donetsk until 2014: Serhiy Stukanov, for example, founded the Ukrainian Conversation Club in 2012, a center for those who wanted to learn or improve their Ukrainian through informal chats. Other conversation clubs followed suit in Nikopol, Horlivka, and Kramatorsk. Other members moved across Ukraine and abroad to build careers and families. It is worth noting that Poshtovkh has given rise to a plethora of Ukrainian journalists: Serhiy Stukalov, Daria Kurennnaya, Valeria Dubova, Oleksandr Demchenko, Oleksandr Khrebet, Daryna Anastasieva, and others.

As is often the case with people—no, People—of this rare type, Yuriy Matushchak's life was a short one. After graduating from the university, Yuriy did a year-long internship in Lublin, and upon returning to Donetsk, he became a schoolteacher, just like Stus, though he taught history rather than Ukrainian language. Amidst the numerous trips, events, and projects organized by Poshtovkh, Matushchak managed to find time to come to Kyiv, where Serhiy Zlyvko lived with his family, to become godfather to his child.

Yuriy was one of the first people to attend the Euromaidan protest in Donetsk, and later, when the war broke out, he joined the Dnipro-1 volunteer battalion. Matushchak and his fellow soldiers were killed in the battle for Illovaisk after being encircled by overwhelming Russian forces in August 2014.

Apartment 4, 32 Shutova Street, Kirovsky district, Donetsk, Donetsk region 83064—this registration address for Poshtovkh can still be found in the state register of legal entities of Ukraine. This is Yuriy's home address in Donetsk, where he lived with his mother and sister. Now, this place exists somewhere in another reality. Yuriy's mother died of cancer. Before the full-scale invasion, his sister and her family lived in Dnipro. The story of Yuriy Matushchak has been

---

14 Interview with Serhiy Stukanov, January 9, 2017.

fictionalized by Oleksandra Ivaniuk based on the accounts of Matushchak's Italian girlfriend, Francesca Leonardi.[15]

***

When Donetsk was occupied in 2014, Donetsk National University was forced to relocate. The new campus happened to be located in Vinnytsia, Stus's home-town, because the city had found a suitable building for the relocated university there. In 2016, the university was finally named after Vasyl Stus. This time, the impetus for the renaming was a letter to the university president on behalf of another graduate of the History Department, Oleksiy Matsuka.[16] Ironically, it was the consequences of the occupation that helped the university change its name: One argument that emerged during the discussions was that renaming it would highlight which university was the *real* one, since the "DPR" had its own so-called "Donetsk National University."

It was also a way to honor the memory of Yuriy Matushchak. In 2016, after the university had been named after Vasyl Stus, a memorial plaque was installed in the university hall in Matushchak's honor.

In 2021, a presentation by the Yuriy Matushchak Journalism Workshop aimed at training future journalists was held in Kramatorsk, with Stanislav Fedorchuk and Serhiy Stukanov among the participants. The journalism workshop was the brainchild of Tetiana Ihnatchenko, a journalist, Euromaidan activist in Mariupol, and head of the Information Department of the Donetsk Regional Military-Civilian Administration.

***

Tetiana Marmazova, the vice president for academic affairs at Donetsk National University at the time of the campaign to rename the university after Vasyl Stus, moved to Russia and became a Russian citizen.[17] Serhiy Baryshnikov, who had supported the so-called Donetsk People's Republic since its earliest days, helped take over the university and became the "acting president" in September 2014, holding this position until the spring of 2015.

***

---

15 The novel "Amor[t]e" was published by XXI Publishing in 2017.

16 See "Istoriia pytannia."

17 "Istoriia pozora: V seti pokazali fanatku 'russkogo mira,' sbezhavshuiu iz Ukrainy" [A story of shame: Pictures of the fan of the "Russian world" who fled Ukraine are now online], *Apostrof*, September 6, 2019, https://apostrophe.ua/ua/news/society/2019-09-06/istoriya-pozora-v-seti-pokazali-fanatku-russkogo-mira-sbejavshuyu-iz-ukrainyi/173803.

The value of Poshtovkh as a phenomenon cannot be overestimated. First of all, the very existence of such an organization shows that a pro-Ukrainian organization in Donetsk could emerge from the grassroots, without government or donor support—it was an example of civil society united around a common goal. Second, Poshtovkh showed that there was demand for the Ukrainian idea in Donbas: as an organization, Poshtovkh created a community of several hundred members and sympathizers, and the number of people who attended its events was steadily growing. Stukanov, Zlyvko, and other members of Poshtovkh are sure that they only needed ten more years: If the attempt to impose the "Russian spring" had taken place in 2024, it would have stood no chance.[18]

---

18 Interestingly, this idea has been echoed by various different people at different times and in different formats: Serhiy Stukanov and Serhiy Zlyvko in interviews with me; Stanislav Fedorchuk in an interview about Euromaidan; and Volodymyr Rafeyenko in his book *Ukraine in Stories and Narratives*.

Chapter 3

The "Interrupted Renaissance" of Donbas: Art as Protest and Protest as Art

In the Soviet myth of Donbas, there was no room for culture (and even less so for Ukrainian and Ukrainian-language culture). In the proletarian community, culture was positioned as something unnecessary, even harmful. The cultural and national revival of the 1920s was quickly suppressed by the Soviet government: in 1940, there were six theaters in the Voroshilovgrad (Luhansk) region, but by 1966, only two of them remained.[1] "The Ukrainian theaters have closed down, and no one misses them. The cultural offerings available to young people are reduced to the guitar, listening to electronic instruments in a restaurant or on a dance floor, or a tape recording. People no longer believe in anything—neither in God nor in the community. Old and not-so-old traditions and rituals have been forgotten, *vechornytsi*,[2] Christmas and New Year's carols, Kupala Night songs[3], etc. have disappeared. And what's left? Mindless sitting in front of a blue screen, going to the movies, drinking, endless talk about football, money, motorbikes, lotteries, off-color tales about sex." This is how Oleksa Tykhyi described cultural life in the Donetsk region in the 1970s.[4]

---

1 Dziuba, *Donets'ka rana Ukrainy*, 6.
2 A traditional evening gathering with music and songs (translator's note).
3 A festival celebrating the summer solstice, where young people wear wreaths and sing and dance around a bonfire (translator's note).
4 Tykhyi, "Dumky pro ridnyi donets'kyi krai."

The situation did not change after Ukraine gained independence: in the early 2000s, there were half as many theaters, cinemas, and clubs in the Donetsk region as in the Lviv region, even though the population of the former was double that of the latter.[5] A telling fact: in 2010, the Luhansk Regional Academic Ukrainian Music and Drama Theater refused to provide a venue for the presentation of Serhiy Zhadan's book *Voroshilovgrad* (as did Donetsk National University; the presentation eventually took place in the Donetsk club *Chicago*). Kharkiv was a cultural hub for young people in Donetsk and Luhansk. In other cities of the Ukrainian East, there was no vibrant cultural life.

Those who craved new cultural experiences had only one option: to create their own alternative. Artistic underground, cultural insurgency, catacomb art—all these metaphors to some extent reflect the new trends that emerged in Donetsk and Luhansk in the 2000s in music, literature, and theater. The New Directors Studio of Alternative Cinematography, which launched the Other Alternative Film Festival, was founded in Donetsk in 2005.[6] There were also several alternative theaters in the city: Beetles, O, and Fifth Wheel. In 2005–2012, Donetsk hosted Art-Alternatyva, an annual festival of alternative theater which brought together professional Ukrainian theaters from Lviv, Kyiv, Odesa, and other cities, as well as amateur and local groups. Poetry slams (impromptu poetry readings) brought a breath of fresh air to the literary world. The idea of protest was a common thread running through most of these cultural trends. And this wasn't just youth protest—the founders and participants of these initiatives were primarily young people born in the late 1980s and early 1990s, so they were the same age as independent Ukraine—but also social and political protest.

These young people didn't call themselves that, nor did they claim to have protest as their goal: they just wanted to do what they loved in a community of like-minded people. But they were essentially continuing the work of Ukrainian dissidents—the work of Mykola Rudenko, Nadiya Svitlychna, Oleksa Tykhyi, Ivan Dziuba, and Vasyl Stus—if by dissidence we mean the creation of Ukrainian culture in a hostile environment. It is no coincidence that these and other dissident human rights activists, members of the Ukrainian Helsinki Group, and

---

5 Bilets'kyi, "Skhid Ukrainy," provides the following data on the number of cultural institutions in the Donetsk and Lviv regions, respectively: theaters—5 and 10; libraries (number of books per 100 people)—1,101 (530) and 1,432 (558); cinemas—156 and 226; clubs—780 and 1,417.

6 Ol'ha Dorovs'kykh, "'Inshi terytorii' Donets'ka" [The other territories of Donetsk], *Radio Svoboda*, December 7, 2009, https://www.radiosvoboda.org/a/1896973.html.

representatives of the Ukrainian Sixtiers generation were born and raised in the Donetsk and Luhansk regions.

The Founder of Donetsk's Poetry Slam

It would be hard to find a more "Donbas" contemporary Ukrainian writer than Oleksiy Chupa: he dreamed up his books at the factory where he worked for seven years, first as a loader and then as a rotary car dumper driver during the formative years of his life, from the age of twenty to twenty-eight. "I'm from an ordinary working-class family, from an ordinary proletarian district in one of the most ordinary cities in Ukraine, a not-quite-Donetsk [Makiivka—K.Z.]": that's how he describes the community where he grew up as a writer. For Chupa, art became an internal act of protest and, at the same time, the creation of a parallel Ukrainian and political identity. Until 2014, Chupa led a double life, working at a factory and fostering a literary community in Donetsk, feeling equally comfortable in both roles.

Chupa recalled the 2007 Lviv Book Forum as one of the most transformative events that defined his approach to literature. During the festival's poetry slam event, the police were called to restrain the poets. In the "poetry spoken under police batons," Chupa recognized a recurring theme for Ukraine: art that the government tries to suppress because it views it as alien and hostile, "a perpetual Sich where ideas are generated." He decided that he had to join in.

Together with his friends Oleksandr Demchenko and Denys Tymoshenko, Oleksiy Chupa went to Lviv for a poetry slam. Inspired by the poetry readings there, he decided that he had to organize something similar in Donetsk. The idea was to bring poets from all over Ukraine to the slam, which would not only signify the high level of the event but would also finally place Donetsk in the national literary context (people say that Ukrainian writers have never traveled to Donbas, and it's true; they haven't been to other places either, but that's another story). Ultimately, only a few authors from Lviv or Kyiv made it; most of the participants were from Donetsk, Luhansk, and Kharkiv. But for Chupa, Demchenko, and others, it was a revelation to see so many people who wrote poetry in the area: the organizers had expected ten participants at most, but more than fifty came.

The poetry slam, which took place on July 5, 2008, was the first in a series of readings: large gatherings with many participants and smaller, intimate readings held every Saturday on the banks of the Kalmius River. The Donetsk slams helped the participants find like-minded people—not just literature and language students, but also engineers from heating plants and waiters from local eateries, who, just like Chupa, largely kept their passion for poetry to themselves. In 2006, only a few people from Donetsk had attended the Independence Day with Makhno literary festival in Huliaypole, but in 2008, two buses full of participants traveled from Donetsk. A community had been forged.

This community was predominantly Russian-speaking. For Donetsk in the early 2000s, this was a normal phenomenon (Volodymyr Rafeyenko wrote in Russian until 2014, and Olena Stiazhkina was nominated for Russian literary awards; Stanislav Aseyev, a representative of the younger generation of Ukrainian writers in Donetsk, also wrote in Russian). But it was a *Ukrainian* community—"a Ukrainian crowd in a Ukrainian setting," as Oleksandr Demchenko described it—and not because it was an organization dedicated to fostering patriotic values (the poetry slams certainly did not pursue this, at least not intentionally), but "by default." The community's Ukrainian identity was not a topic of discussion because it was never in doubt.

At the same time, the community wasn't just about art: it was also about one's civic position. For example, in 2011, the Postup Human Rights Center in Luhansk launched a slam tournament as a protest against the Law on the Protection of Public Morality, which artists considered to be an attack on freedom of speech and the establishment of censorship.[7]

The Donetsk poetry slams continued until 2014. With the Russian invasion, everything stopped: some people went to fight, some became volunteers, some left, and some stayed in the occupied territories. Chupa says no one from the community took a pro-Russian stance. For him, 2014 was a year of literary recognition: three of his books of prose were published (*Ten Words About Homeland*, *The Homeless of Donbas*, and *Tales of My Bomb Shelter*), and he self-published a poetry collection, *Comma*. His books were longlisted for the BBC Ukraine Book of the Year Award and translated into several European languages. The Polish translation of *Ten Words About Homeland* was nominated for the 2017 Angelus Award.

Chupa has since ceased writing books. He has grown disillusioned with the effectiveness of literature and believes that weapons are now more important.

Demchenko has also stopped writing poetry. At the time of writing, he was working for Radio Svoboda (Liberty) on the "Donbas. Realities" project. He wants to write a pamphlet titled "Why I Chose Ukraine" for those who stayed in the occupied territories of the Donetsk and Luhansk regions.[8]

---

7 "Slem-turnir za svobodu slova" [A slam tournament for freedom of speech], Litaktsent, April 12, 2011, http://litakcent.com/2011/04/12/slem-turnir-za-svobodu-slova/.

8 At the time of the preparation of the book's English version (Fall 2024), Demchenko is serving in the Armed Forces of Ukraine (author's note).

An excerpt from an unpublished novel by Chupa and some of Demchenko's poems were included in *A Rock: An Anthology of Ukrainian Writers of Donbas*, published in 2017 and edited by Stanislav Fedorchuk. The anthology features works by over sixty authors from different generations, writing in Ukrainian and Russian, both well-known and emerging writers, but all from the Donetsk and Luhansk regions. Ivan Dziuba wrote the introduction as if passing the baton to younger generations of writers. Dziuba, the last representative of the Sixtiers generation in the Donetsk region, passed away on February 22, 2022, two days before Russia's full-scale invasion of Ukraine. It was as if he was telling us: "Our fight is over. Now it's your turn."

Luhansk's STAN: Art Against the Regime

When Yaroslav Minkin, a Luhansk native who'd spent his childhood and teen-age years in Crimea because of his father's sudden decision to move somewhere warmer, returned to Luhansk at the age of seventeen, he experienced what we would call a culture shock. Yaroslav was seriously interested in literature: he'd even won "republic-wide"[9] literary competitions and considered himself reasonably well-read. But in Luhansk, he met people whose reading abilities were vastly superior to his—people who could devour two thousand pages in a week. He once recalled how a writer from Molodohvardiysk invited him over. The host's home struck Minkin as very humble—the family of three shared two spoons and one fork—yet it was filled with books and translated notes and records.[10] His host was Oleksandr Sihida, a Luhansk writer and founder of the STAN art association.

STAN, the art community that came together around Sihida, was an act of resistance to the urban culture of Luhansk at the time. This confrontation—art as protest and protest as art—defined the group's work throughout its existence.

A distinctive feature of STAN was that it attracted people of very different ideological backgrounds. It brought together Ukrainian and Russian speakers, national democrats, communists, and radicals of all kinds. It was a co-existence, communication, and community that is difficult to imagine from the perspective of the radicalized "bubbles" of the twenty-first century. It included writers, musicians, artists, and activists from Luhansk and other regions of Ukraine: the

---

9   In Crimea, this term was used to refer to events that were held within the Autonomous Republic of Crimea.

10 Interview with Yaroslav Minkin, February 4, 2021.

poets Kostiantyn Skorkin and Lyubov Yakimchuk, Yaroslav Minkin, Kostiantyn Reutskyi, the artist Viacheslav Bondarenko, and many others.

STAN as an art community was doubly marginalized: on the one hand, as a group of creative people in an industrial, sometimes even anti-creative environment; on the other, as a community of primarily Russian-speaking artists in a country where becoming part of the larger nationwide literary community necessitated writing in Ukrainian.

Instead, the group communicated and wrote mainly in Russian (the acronym "STAN" is actually an abbreviation of the founders' self-irony: *samye talantlivye avtory nashi*, or "Our most talented authors"). There were exceptions, of course. Some STAN members were bilingual: for example, they spoke Russian in their daily lives but wrote poetry in Ukrainian or both languages. Some authors, such as Lyubov Yakimchuk, belonged to the Ukrainian-speaking section of the group.

At the same time, even though Luhansk artists wrote in Russian, this didn't automatically mean that they embraced Russian culture—contact with contemporary Russian authors was more occasional than systematic. Their literary icons were Serhiy Zhadan and Yuriy Pokalchuk (incidentally, Pokalchuk was the first Ukrainian-language writer of note to come to Luhansk on a book tour), not their Russian counterparts. *Ukrainian Week* journalist Bohdan Butkevych, who wrote about STAN back in 2010, remarked with astonishment: "They continue to believe in the future of Ukrainian culture while living in conditions that are brutally hostile to any culture."[11] In terms of social activism, the members of STAN were clearly influenced by Russian trends, although they did not copy them but creatively adapted them instead.

For example, they were influenced by the art collective Voina (some of whose members later joined the Pussy Riot group), which organized provocative art performances in Moscow.[12] Inspired by their example, in 2008 STAN members organized the Uprising (VosSTANie) Art Terrorist Festival. This involved a symbolic hijacking of a tram: paintings were hung, poets recited poetry, and musicians performed in an actual Luhansk tram as it traveled along its usual route.[13] This is how STAN members expressed their protest against a plan announced by the mayor to dismantle tramlines in Luhansk.

---

11 Butkevych, "Literaturni povstantsi Dalekoho Skhodu."
12 Interview with Yaroslav Minkin, February 4, 2021.
13 Svitlana Oslavs'ka, "Luhans'k, iakoho nemaie. Reportazh 'Zaborony' pro pidpil'nu kul'turu naiskhidnishoho mista Ukrainy" [The Luhansk that no longer exists. *Zaborona*'s reportage on the underground culture of Ukraine's easternmost city], *Zaborona*, June 30, 2020, https://zaborona.com/lugansk-yakogo-nemaye/.

The themes of revolution, terror, war, and anarchy kept coming up in STAN's work as a recurrent narrative: members of the group burned their writers' union membership cards and declared a civil war in the category of esthetic content, and the governing body of STAN was called the "Revolutionary Military Council." Despite the revolutionary romance that inspired STAN members, these linguistic markers served only non-violent purposes and were purely performative. The "hijacking" of the tram was carried out in line with the best democratic standards: the organization informed the local authorities about the event in advance and asked law enforcement agencies for protection.[14]

STAN's activism is notable for this combination of symbolic violence, violence as inspiration, and exclusively peaceful actions, and for the exemplary democratic coexistence between the community and local authorities in the region, which was widely considered almost the property of the Party of Regions and its leader Oleksandr Yefremov. Yaroslav Minkin, one of STAN's leaders, recalled that at one point protests organized by STAN members were being held almost weekly, but the authorities never resisted. Minkin says this is because STAN's actions were, first of all, relatively small scale, and secondly, so frequent that the local police simply got used to them.

Additionally, during the protests, the group never issued any demands or an agenda with recommendations for the authorities. The campaigns they organized were somewhat anarchic against the regime as such, and the historical icon of many STAN members was Nestor Makhno.[15] At some point, STAN's protest agenda lost its thematic boundaries: they protested against everything from the closure of second-hand stores to the appointment of Dmytro Tabachnyk as Minister of Education and Science.

And yet STAN members got away with openly satirizing the current government—such as when they created the Yanukona, a pseudo-icon of Viktor Yanukovych made out of empty Svitoch candy boxes in 2011 by artist Viacheslav Bondarenko (Slava Bo).[16] STAN members recall that the irony was misunderstood only in Kyiv, where the artwork was perceived as a literal act of

---

14 Interview with Yaroslav Minkin, February 4, 2021.

15 It is worth noting that this is not only a coincidence of ideological preferences, but also a historical coincidence: as Stanislav Kulchytskyi and Larysa Yakubova have pointed out, "Primacy among the socio-political forces that searched for the ways and place of Donbas in the revolutionary liberation movements of 1917–1920 rightfully belonged to the anarchist peasant movement led by Nestor Makhno, which grew into an independent political camp of all-Ukrainian significance [. . .]. In fact, it was a historical inversion of the idea of Cossack freedom, which is inherently characteristic of Ukrainians." Kul'chyts'kyi and Yakubova, *Trysta rokiv samotnosti*, 138.

16 Oslavs'ka, "Luhans'k, iakoho nemaie."

worship for the president from Donbas.[17] As for the local authorities, they were simply too self-assured to feel threatened by what looked like merely a bunch of freaks to the Luhansk of that time.

Over time, STAN evolved into a "classic" NGO until it was officially registered in 2008. The founders of the STAN NGO were Yaroslav Minkin, Olena Zaslavska, and Kostiantyn Skorkin. STAN's art wing was slowly declining: Oleksandr Sihida started drinking and came to Luhansk less and less often, while the STAN NGO turned to more professionalized activities, becoming a partner of the Docudays festival, developing a Cultural Map of Luhansk, putting together an anthology against gender-based violence titled *From Victims to Liquidators*, and so on.

While ideology had rarely been the cause of rifts before 2014 (except in 2004, when even STAN was affected by a degree of radicalization), after Russia's hybrid aggression, all the members of the community had to make a choice. Oleksandr Sihida stayed in the so-called "Luhansk People's Republic" ("LPR") and became a member of their Writers' Union. The poet Olena Zaslavska also joined the "LPR," surprising her former friends. Kostiantyn Skorkin moved to Moscow and now writes for the Carnegie Moscow Center.

STAN still exists today. It is headed by Yaroslav Minkin, who moved to Ivano-Frankivsk in 2014. Now, it is a youth NGO that specializes in non-formal education in human rights, cultural management, democratic practices, and other areas.[18]

Lyubov Yakimchuk has built probably the most successful literary career of all the STAN authors: she has won many literary awards, including Ukraine's *Koronatsiia slova* award. In 2015, the Old Lion Publishing House published her collection of poems about the war, *Apricots of Donbas*.[19]

Kostiantyn Reutskyi worked for Vostok SOS, a volunteer organization based in Kyiv's Pechersk district. He is reluctant to discuss his literary work. He is more concerned with human rights, a cause to which he has devoted more than 20 years of his life. Until 2014, he was the leader of the Postup human rights organization in Luhansk. After the full-scale invasion, he joined the Armed Forces of Ukraine.

---

17 Interview with Yaroslav Minkin, February 4, 2021.
18 STAN's team is now based in Ivano-Frankivsk. The organization's website is stan.org.ua.
19 Available in English from Lost Horse Press in a translation by Oksana Maksymchuk, Max Rosochinsky, and Svetlana Lavochkina (translator's note).

Slava Bo was a prisoner of the "LPR" terrorist organization. After his release, he moved to Kyiv and, as of 2021, he was publishing a magazine about the culture of the Luhansk region, *PlusMinusInfinite*.[20]

Izolyatsia: A Reinterpretation

Kyiv and Ivano-Frankivsk were not the first cities in Ukraine to start giving old industrial spaces a new life, turning them into creative hubs, fairgrounds, and trendy venues. The first city to do this was Donetsk.

The Izolyatsia Foundation was founded in Donetsk in 2010 on the basis of a factory which made mineral wool, a raw material for insulation. The factory opened in 1955 and continued to operate until 2005. The idea of turning the closed, bankrupt factory into a contemporary art center came from Lyubov Mykhailova and her daughter Viktoria Ivanova, the daughter and granddaughter of the long-time director Ivan Mykhailov, who ran the factory for fifty years.

Lyubov Mykhailova grew up in Donetsk, but in the 1990s she left Ukraine and lived in various countries, including Greece, Austria, and Canada. While living in the West, she became interested in philanthropy and was inspired by examples of former industrial spaces that had been revitalized through culture and art. In one of her interviews, Mykhailova recounted how in 2010, she visited the Zollverein in Essen, Germany, and saw a coking plant that had been transformed into a cultural space: "It was like a lightning strike. It was still industrial heritage, but no one had plundered it or cut it up for scrap. It had been revitalized, given a new life, just as industrialization once gave new life to Donbas."[21]

This was the objective that the founders of the Izolyatsia Foundation tried to accomplish: reviving the factory as a center of social life in Donetsk, not through industry, but through culture. At first, the director of the factory, Ivan Mykhailov, was skeptical of his daughter's idea. Eventually he was convinced, including by economic arguments: a new identity for the factory meant new jobs.

---

20 Sergei Gorelov, "Vot i Slava Bo. Kak s nulevym biudzhetom i v krizis sozdat' zhurnal o kul'ture Luganshchiny" [Here comes Slava Bo. How to create a magazine about the culture of the Luhansk region with a non-existing budget and during a crisis], Svoi.City, April 30, 2020, https://svoi.city/read/history/77991/65plyus-minus-beskonechnost.

21 Anastasiia Platonova and Dar'ia Badior, "Liubov Mykhailova: 'Tam, de nemaie kul'tury, ale ie televizor i RPTs, krytychno vazhlyvo praciuvaty z liud'my'" [Lyubov Mykhailova: "Where there is no culture, but there are TVs and the Russian Orthodox Church, it's vital to work with people"], LB.ua, March 26, 2020, https://lb.ua/culture/2020/03/26/453552_lyubov_mihaylova_tam_gde.html.

The Izolyatsia Foundation: Platform for Cultural Initiatives was the first institution in Donetsk to work systematically with contemporary culture and art, arranging exhibitions, events, and festivals. Before that, similar events in the city had only ever been organized by foreign diplomatic missions: the "French Spring" sponsored by the French Embassy in Ukraine, Polish Film Days, etc.

From the very first events, it became clear that there was great interest locally in the Foundation's work: more people came to their talks, which were temporarily held at the Art Museum, than there were seats. The quality of the content was only part of the reason, the other part being the lack of alternatives: the Izolyatsia team used to joke that the Foundation had only two competitors in Donetsk: the Donbas Arena (the sports stadium) and Donetsk-City (a shopping mall).

It was important for the foundation not to alienate what was local but to engage with it. This intention was embodied in its very name: although from today's perspective it may seem that the name "Izolyatsia" alluded to the isolation and alienation of the Donetsk region from the cultural context of the rest of Ukraine, it was actually just a play on the name of the factory's insulation products.

The themes addressed by the foundation were also grounded in the local context. For example, Izolyatsia invited the Chinese American artist Cai Guo-Qiang to create portraits of miners, which he made using gunpowder. Another example is the installation *Lipstick*, created in 2012 by the Cameroonian-Belgian artist Pascale Marthine Tayou, who dedicated it to the women of Donbas. A giant metallic red lipstick was installed on top of a factory chimney.[22]

Izolyatsia refused to take any money from politicians or oligarchs. For Mykhailova, it was a non-profit project: she invested her own money in it and fundraised for it. An international cultural institution with a transparent budget and accountability—that was another innovation that the Foundation brought to the Donetsk region.

Over the four years of its existence, the Foundation grew into a powerful enough organization to become a nuisance to the local authorities. In April 2013, just as Izolyatsia was hosting a seminar with US Ambassador John Tefft, it was attacked by the "Donetsk People's Republic," then a marginalized

---

22 Taisiia Bakhareva, "Anna Medvedeva: 'Nashu installiatsiiu "Pomada" v Donetske boeviki razrushili ogromnym kolichestvom vzryvchatki'" [Anna Medvedeva: "Militants Destroyed Our *Lipstick* Installation in Donetsk with a Huge Amount of Explosives"], *Fakty*, July 9, 2015, https://fakty.ua/202511-anna-medvedeva-nashu-installyaciyu-pomada-v-donecke-boeviki-razrushili-ogromnym-kolichestvom-vzryvchatki.

non-government organization.[23] Foundation team members say the attackers were assisted by the local police and Roman Liahin, who was affiliated with the Party of Regions. Lyubov Mykhailova recalled how Liahin, a frequent visitor to Izolyatsia, once told her: "Now I know: if we were back in Soviet times, you would have been put in prison long ago for undermining the social order."[24] In 2012, ArtDonbass, an art gallery which remained loyal to the local authorities, was founded to counterbalance the Isolyatsia Foundation.[25]

The Izolyatsia Foundation positioned itself as an apolitical organization—at that time, being "apolitical" meant not having direct ties with political parties. The Foundation considered itself a "territory of liberal democracy," so when the Revolution of Dignity began, its support was unequivocal. The Foundation team was unsure how common this stance was in Donetsk: Mykhailo Hlubokyi, Izolyatsia's Development Director, used to avoid discussing the Revolution with his friends so that he would not be disappointed to learn their views. An event organized by the Foundation in the winter of 2013, a Christmas fair, helped to identify like-minded people. In addition to selling locally made crafts and Christmas foods, the fair was also a place where videos from the Maidan were shown and items brought from Kyiv featuring Ukrainian and European symbols were handed out—visitors gladly accepted them and were photographed with them. Hlubokyi noted that it was this fair that showed him how many like-minded people there were in Donetsk.[26]

On April 23–25, 2014, when Donetsk was already occupied, Izolyatsia hosted a Ukrainian Literary Festival, the first literary event of this scale in Donetsk. Among the participants were Lyubko Deresh, Yuriy Vynnychuk, Irena Karpa, Mark Livin, Kateryna Babkina, and other celebrities of contemporary Ukrainian literature. The event had been planned before the Russian invasion, but as the "Russian Spring" unfolded in the region, the Foundation's team decided to hold the festival as an act of cultural protest against the "voice of Donbas" that the occupiers were attempting to impose and pass off as genuine.

The festival took place as planned, but it was the first and last event the organizers managed to hold in Donetsk. Lyubov Mykhailova received threats, and for

23 Oleksandr Lashchenko, "Potekhin: 'Izoliaciia'—eto deistvuiushchii sovremennyi kontslager'" [Potekhin: "Izolyatsia is a Functioning Modern Concentration Camp"], Radio Svoboda, September 4, 2019, https://www.radiosvoboda.org/a/donbass-realii/30144941.html.

24 "Liubov' Mikhailova: Izoliatsiia byla zanozoi na tele Donbassa, poskol'ku uchila liudei dumat'" [Lyubov Mykhailova: Izolyatsia was a thorn in Donbas's side because it taught people to think], ART UKRAINE, June 17, 2014, https://artukraine.com.ua/a/lyubov-mikhaylo-va--izolyaciya-byla-zanozoy-na-tele-donbassa-poskolku-uchila-lyudey-dumat/.

25 "O muzee" [About the museum], Artdonbass.ru, http://artdonbass.ru/ru/page/o-muzee.html.

26 Interview with Mykhailo Hlubokyi, April 29, 2022.

safety reasons, she decided to hold a strategic planning meeting with her team in Kyiv. On June 9, the day the team members gathered in the capital, they learned that Russia-backed proxies had taken over the Foundation. Mykhailova noted that the takeover was led by Liahin, who became the "minister of social affairs" of the "DPR."

The taking over of Izolyatsia could not have been a coincidence. The reason wasn't just that the Foundation's facilities were especially suitable for the militants' needs. The values the Foundation shared and actively promoted—critical thinking, innovation, proactivity, and democracy—directly conflicted with the order that the Kremlin puppets were trying to impose.

The art space was converted into a prison and torture chamber,[27] and its story is told by one of its former prisoners, Stanislav Aseyev, in his book *The Torture Camp on Paradise Street*.[28] The metaphor inherent in the Foundation's name, "Isolation," had acquired another meaning—this time, a sinister one. Most of the artworks were destroyed by the occupiers: *Lipstick* was blown up with explosives, sculptures were used for target practice, anything that could be utilized for scrap was dismantled.[29]

***

Since 2014, the Izolyatsia Foundation has been based in Kyiv. The team continued the idea of transforming an industrial zone into a creative hub: in Kyiv, the Foundation rents the premises of a former factory in Podil, where IZONE, a coworking space, has been created. The Izolyatsia Foundation has also established a Donbas Studies program, which includes a library, research, and a public program for artists.

The Foundation continued its work in the small towns of the Donetsk and Luhansk regions and opened an office (which the Foundation refers to as its "home base") in Soledar, the city where Cai Guo-Qiang's *1040 Meters under the Earth* project began. After Russia's full-scale invasion, the Izolyatsia Foundation channeled all its resources into support for communities and people affected by the war and supporting cultural resistance.

***

27 "Strakh ta smert' v 'Izoliatsii'. Iak katuiut' liudei u pidvalakh Donets'ka" [Fear and death in 'Isolation'. How people are tortured in Donetsk's basements], *Ukrains'ka pravda*, February 24, 2020, https://www.pravda.com.ua/articles/2020/02/24/7241046/.

28 Available in English from HURI in a translation by Zenia Tompkins and Nina Murray (translator's note).

29 Bakhareva, "Anna Medvedeva."

Donetsk's Izolyatsia was not the only art space the Russian invaders turned into a murder weapon. In 2022, they targeted the Mariupol Drama Theater (full name: Donetsk Regional Academic Drama Theater) and more than a thousand civilians who were hiding there from the shelling and bombs. The Drama Theater, founded in 1878, was the oldest theater in the Donetsk region. Its walls had witnessed performances by Panas Saksahanskyi and Ivan Karpenko-Karyi and the theater groups of Marko Kropyvnytskyi and Mykhailo Starytskyi. Between the Russian occupation in 2014 and the beginning of the full-scale invasion in 2022, the Drama Theater was the only one of the five theaters in the Donetsk region that was still open in Ukrainian-controlled territory.

On March 16, 2022, Russian forces launched an airstrike on the theater. At the time, over a thousand civilians were sheltering there—just as in the Middle Ages, when people would seek refuge in churches, but in this case, it was a temple of the arts. Associated Press estimates that about 600 civilians were killed.[30]

On the day of the airstrike, according to a poster predating the war, the theater would have been presenting the play *Dissenting and Unconquered* in memory of Oleksa Tykhyi, a Ukrainian dissident from the Donetsk region and co-founder of the Ukrainian Helsinki Group.[31]

---

30 Lori Hinnant, Mstyslav Chernov, and Vasilisa Stepanenko, "Evidence Points to 600 Dead in Mariupol Theater Airstrike," AP News, May 4, 2022, https://apnews.com/article/russia-ukraine-war-mariupol-theater-c321a196fbd568899841b506afcac7a1?utm_%20medium=AP&utm_campaign=SocialFlow&utm_source=Twitter.

31 "Dramteatr Mariupolia razbombili. Segodnia zdes' dolzhna byla byt' prem'era 'Nezgidnoho ta neskorenoho'" [Mariupol drama theater bombed. The premier of *Dissenting and Unconquered* would have taken place here today], Svoi.City, March 16, 2022, https://svoi.city/articles/199168/dramteatr-v-mariupole-razbombili.

Chapter 4

The Outskirts of Europe: Does European Donbas Exist?

————

To get to Lysychansk, we drove from Sievierodonetsk with a local driver. In 2018, Lysychansk received a 2017 Belgian Heritage Abroad Award from the King Baudouin Foundation: out of thirty-three buildings that Belgian investors and entrepreneurs built at the turn of the nineteenth and the twentieth centuries, about thirty had survived. We joked about it along the way: my fellow travelers, displaced Donetsk residents, could not believe that European "ruins" could be of interest to anyone. The local driver himself did not know exactly where the objects of our interest—a Belgian hospital and a gymnasium (secondary school)—were located. Using our phones, we showed him photos of the red brick buildings and craned our necks trying to spot them from the car windows.

Eventually we found the hospital, at 3 Mohylevska Street, on an overgrown hill. But its condition could hardly have been described as anything other than deplorable: until recently, one could at least admire its elegant facade, dubbed "the Ukrainian Hogwarts," but now the view was obscured by a green safety fence. The fence was ostensibly installed to protect the building from vandals, but the precautions did not work: in May 2021, a fire broke out and destroyed the roof of the building. In the last decade, a number of interesting books and articles have appeared about the European heritage of Donbas,[1] but the situation

---

1 The most famous works include Wim Peeters's *Steel on the Steppe* (2010) and Valentyna Lazebnyk's *Steel on the Steppe. A View from Ukraine* (Art Press, 2017). Among the articles, I

in Lysychansk perfectly illustrates the current situation: while more and more people are learning about the European roots of industrial Donbas, they have fewer and fewer chances to see the European heritage with their own eyes. The Belgian hospital closed in 1995, which means that for more than twenty-five years the building has been gradually deteriorating: there are plenty of photos on the Internet showing its condition worsening year on year. As of 2018, only two buildings out of the three dozen had architectural monument status, and the rest were not even on the city's balance sheet.[2]

The history of the European Union famously began with the establishment of a controlling body over the coal and metals industries of France and Germany, who had been enemies in the Second World War. As it happened, it was coal and steel that brought Europe to the Ukrainian land of Donbas, literally turning the region into a European union of coal and steel, as well as glass, soda, and other industrial sectors. Hiroaki Kuromiya called Donbas "Russia's and Ukraine's Ruhr" (by analogy with the Ruhr, the largest coal basin in Western Europe, located in Germany),[3] while Wim Peeters called the region "the Russian Seraing" (by analogy with Seraing, the center of Belgium's metals industry).[4]

In a previous chapter, I cited Lenin's pronouncement that "Donbas [. . .] is a region without which the building of socialism will remain merely a good intention." Yet it is not the Soviet government that needs to be credited for the development of the region's industrial potential. European colonizers were the first to develop and exploit the industrial potential of this area in the late nineteenth century when the region was part of the Russian Empire. Valentyna Lazebnyk quotes the late nineteenth-century Russian historian Boris Brandt, who wrote: "If foreigners had not come to the rescue with their capital and their

recommend reading Svitlana Oslavs'ka and Anna Il'chenko, "Stara Ievropa Donbasu" [The old Europe of Donbas], *The Ukrainians*, June 4, 2018, https://theukrainians.org/donbaska-yevropa/, as well as Tetiana Matychak's English-language article "Europe's Donbas: How Western Capital Industrialized Eastern Ukraine" (2019) for *Ukraine World*, https://ukraineworld.org/en/articles/ukraine-explained/europes-donbas-how-western-capital-industrialized-eastern-ukraine. In 2022, Korniy Hrytsiuk's documentary *EuroDonbas* was released (you can watch the trailer at https://www.facebook.com/watch/?v=951638722188978).

2 According to Nina Bondar, director of the Lysychansk City Museum of Local History (Ivanka Mishchenko, "Lysychans'k otrymav premiiu Fondu korolia Belhii" [Lysychansk receives King Baudouin Foundation award], *Uriadovyi kur'ier*, March 3, 2018, https://ukurier.gov.ua/uk/articles/lisichansk-otrimav-premiyu-fondu-korolya-belgiyi/).

3 Kuromiya, *Freedom and Terror in the Donbas*, 14.

4 Wim Peeters, *Stal' u stepu* [Steel on the steppe], trans. Dmytro Chystiak (Kyiv: Tempora, 2010), 24.

entrepreneurship, which does not stop even in the face of a recognized risk . . . the South of Russia might still be fast asleep."[5]

Western Europeans laid the foundations for the future "industrial pride" of Donbas: in 1865, Welsh entrepreneur John Hughes began the mining history of Yuzivka (now Donetsk); in 1895, the Austrian Land Bank (Länderbank) and the French company Société Générale founded the Makiivka Coal Company; in 1899, Donetsk Glass and Chemical Factories, incorporated as a Belgian Société Anonyme, established an enterprise that later became the pride of Donbas—the Avtosklo factory in Kostiantynivka; the Russian-Belgian company Lyubimov, Solve & Co. founded a soda factory in Lysychansk which ceased operations only in 2011; in 1900, the Luhansk Steam Locomotive Factory, founded by the German industrialist Gustav Hartmann, began operating. The list could go on. Luhansk, Druzhkivka, Yenakiyevo, Selydove, Mariupol, Debaltseve, Torez, Kramatorsk, and other cities in the present-day Donetsk and Luhansk regions of Ukraine have also been the recipients of European investment.[6]

The region can be broadly divided into four "spheres of influence": the so-called Belgian province with its center in Luhansk, the German land in the south of the Donetsk region, the French area in the east, and the English area in the center.[7] Hiroaki Kuromiya noted: "On the eve of World War I, twenty-six of the thirty-six joint-stock companies in the Donbas coal-mining industry had almost exclusively foreign capital. These firms yielded [. . .] more than 70 percent of all coal production in the Donbas."[8] At the beginning of the twentieth century, only St. Petersburg had more foreign consulates than Mariupol.[9] In addition, by 1917, the region was producing 87% of the country's coal, 70% of its iron, 57% of steel, more than 90% of coke, and more than 60% of soda and mercury.[10]

Perhaps the best-known story of the European colonization of Donbas is British—or, more precisely, Welsh—one associated with the industrialist John Hughes. This industrialist was in fact the first to come to develop this promising region. Hughes started from scratch: before he arrived, there were only a few

5   Valentyna Lazebnyk, *Stal' u stepu. Pohliad z Ukrainy* [Steel on the steppe. A view from Ukraine] (Dnipro: Art Press, 2017), 227.
6   Matychak, "Europe's Donbas."
7   Ibid.
8   Kuromiya, *Freedom and Terror in the Donbas*, 49.
9   Vikhrov, *Dykyi skhid*, 70.
10 Anatolii Mykhnenko, *Istoriia Donbasu (1861–1945)* [The history of Donbas (1861–1945)] (Donetsk: Iugo-vostok, 1999), 11, 23, 50. Quoted in Studenna-Skrukwa, *Ukrains'kyi Donbas*, 230.

small mines in Donbas that employed few workers.[11] At the time, due to low or even zero-rated duties, the Russian Empire imported foreign coal, including British coal.[12] Researcher Marta Studenna-Skrukwa lists other reasons for the insignificant use of Donetsk coal in the early nineteenth century: the lack of convenient transportation routes between Donbas and Black Sea ports; the underdeveloped railway network, lack of capital and resources, and so on.[13]

In the 1860s, however, incentives for foreign capital began to appear: the Russian government's policy changed significantly with the start of railroad construction and the abolition of serfdom. It was then that Hughes proposed a plan for the development of the Donetsk basin to the tsarist government. In 1869, he founded the New Russian Coal, Iron, and Rail-making Company, an English-Russian joint-stock company. Three years later, in 1872, the first blast furnace, built by Welsh specialists, was launched.[14] Hughes's enterprises gradually began to transform into an industrial empire that included a metallurgical plant, mines, almost 500 miles of railroad track, bridges, locomotive depots, and, by 1886, 64 commercial and industrial establishments ranging from bakeries and taverns to bathhouses.[15] Within twenty-five years, the New Russia Company had turned into an "industrial giant of Russia."[16] In 1869, at the time of its founding, the population of Yuzivka was 6,000 people; by 1894 it was 50,000.[17] In 1913, 74% of the Russian Empire's steel was produced in Yuzivka.[18]

It was Hughes's example that inspired other Western Europeans to invest in the region. In 1886, the Belgian company Cockerill founded the South-Russian Dnipro Metallurgical Company, which became a symbol of Belgian industrial development.[19] It is a telling fact that in the early twentieth century, Belgium was the first and main foreign investor in the Russian Empire (among the "Big Four": along with France, Germany, and Britain), and two-thirds of all its investments were in the Donetsk coal basin.[20] Between 1895 and 1901, 117 joint-stock companies were founded in the Russian Empire, 60 of which operated in the territory of present-day Ukraine. The connection between Belgium and Donbas was so strong that there was a direct train from Yekaterynoslav (now

---

11 Studenna-Skrukwa, *Ukrains'kyi Donbas*, 227.
12 Ibid, 228.
13 Ibid, 228–229.
14 Piters, *Stal' u stepu*, 13.
15 Kul'chyts'kyi and Yakubova, *Trysta rokiv samotnosti*, 66–67.
16 Studenna-Skrukwa, *Ukrains'kyi Donbas*, 231.
17 Peeters, *Stal' u stepu*, 13.
18 Matychak, "Europe's Donbas."
19 Peeters, *Stal' u stepu*, 14.
20 Ibid.

Dnipro) to Brussels, which took 65 hours, and Belgium referred to Donbas as its "tenth province."[21]

Europeans moved to Donbas, taking their whole families with them—not only did they receive promotions, housing, higher salaries, and opportunities that were not available to them at home, they were also "helping" their employer by agreeing to move to the distant and unknown East.[22] European culture—theaters, casinos, clubs, schools, and hospitals—arrived together with the Europeans.

Yet the arrival of "Europe" in Donbas should not be idealized, as it was mostly inaccessible to the local population. While the Belgians, for example, lived in specially built brick houses with electricity and running water and enjoyed the available entertainment infrastructure—the theater, dance hall, casino, etc.—the living conditions of the local population were radically different from those of the foreigners. Stanislav Kulchytskyi and Larysa Yakubova note that despite the fact that Donbas seemed like an industrial giant compared to other regions of Ukraine and the Russian Empire, "the distance between Donbas and its Western European 'brothers' remained civilizational in all its components: social, cultural, and mental."[23] They also cite the following statistics: "On the eve of the First World War, 40.4% of miners lived in dugouts without windows and floors, 2.5% lived in sheds and summer kitchens, 25.8% lived in peasant huts, and only 22.3% lived in brick and stone houses."[24] Broadly speaking, there were two residential areas in Yuzivka: the English Colony and the Russian Quarter, also dubbed "Shanghai" or "Dog Houses" because of the poor living conditions.[25] Theodore Friedgut, a professor of Slav Studies at Jerusalem University who is cited by Hiroaki Kuromiya, mentions another level of stratification—between the factory workers, who were closer to modern urban culture, and the miners, who were at a lower level.[26] Moreover, a system like the one established by John Hughes, where there was a zone of influence in which he was the sole person to make decisions on all issues, substituting himself for the state, is essentially a prototype of the "legalized lawlessness" that post-Soviet oligarchs have practiced for over a century.

---

21 At the time, Belgium had nine provinces. Source: Matychak, "Europe's Donbas."
22 Peeters, *Stal' u stepu*, 37.
23 Kul'chyts'kyi and Yakubova, *Trysta rokiv samotnosti*, 70.
24 Ibid, 93.
25 Studenna-Skrukwa, *Ukrains'kyi Donbas*, 234.
26 Theodore Friedgut, *Iuzovka and Revolution*, vol. 1: *Life and Work in Russia's Donbass, 1869–1924* (Princeton, NJ: Princeton University Press, 1989), 330. Quoted in Kuromiya, *Freedom and Terror in the Donbas*, 52.

The social differentiation was most clearly illustrated by the remuneration of foreign and local workers and the positions they could hold. Wim Peeters presented the following comparative table:

Table 2. Belgians in the Russian Empire by qualification and salary level (1897–1898)[27]

Work type (Belgian workers)	Salary per year (in gold francs)	Work type (Russian and Ukrainian workers)	Salary per year (in gold francs)
Smelting shop worker	1,262	Blast furnace worker	1,110—1,170
Steel sheet production worker	4,745—9,490	Steel mill worker	1,210—1,260
Steel mill worker	5,825	Enterprise employee	1,360—1,460
Enterprise employee	3,600—4,800	Rail production worker	1,460—1,550
Rail production worker	11,650—27,300	Miner	1,970
Other workers	3,600—4,800		
Foreman	4,343—11,170		
Department head	15,000—18,000		
Administrative officer	16,000—30,000		
Engineer	15,000—50,000		
Manager	40,000—150,000		
General director	80,000—100,000		

There were objective reasons for this salary inequality: workers from Western Europe had the required qualifications, while local workers were unskilled and trained by foreigners.

Yet the differences were not limited to the wages: they also manifested themselves in the attitude toward the local population. According to

---

27 Piters, *Stal' u stepu*, 37.

treated the locals as a disenfranchised workforce.
quotes Anatoliy Mykhnenko: "They behaved
[. . .] towards the Russian workers, pushing and
ting them up; if anyone protested, the foremen
...sguising their lawlessness, resorted to one of the
...ing them of piecework earnings [. . .]; arbitrary fining
...orkers who complained to the factory inspector, etc."[28]
...hn Hughes's empire was subordinate solely to him: "neither
...ie city council (local government) nor the governor's representative (state administration) operated on its territory."[29] When workers wanted to leave, Hughes would refuse to return their internal passports, and he ordered the railway station master not to sell tickets to those who did not have a passport.[30] At the same time, "once conflict occurred, savage force was used; and workers were flogged as if they were children and slaves whose misbehavior ought to be corrected by paternal whipping."[31] Another striking quote from Kuromiya's book is this: "Mortality among the Hughes workers significantly exceeds that among prisoners in the Siberian mines."[32] Hughes's was not the only enterprise to treat workers as if they were semi-slaves: this was also typical of other Europeans.[33] The bitter irony was that the abolition of serfdom in the Russian Empire was one of the factors that enabled the inflow of foreign capital to Donbas, but the arrival of foreign capital essentially prolonged the existence of the feudal serf system in the industrial East.

The history of European capital in Donbas ended as swiftly as it had begun. When the First World War broke out, the tsarist government used it as a pretext to redirect the work of enterprises to serve the needs of the war economy, and the 1917 Revolution put an end to the presence of Western capital in the USSR—the Soviets simply nationalized it, or, in other words, illegally appropriated it. For this reason, Belgium would not recognize the Soviet Union until 1935.

---

28 Mykhnenko, *Istoriia Donbasu*, 35–36. Quoted in Studenna-Skrukwa, *Ukrains'kyi Donbas*, 238. Hiroaki Kuromiya has also noted the European employers' brutal attitude toward the local workers (Kuromiya, *Freedom and Terror in the Donbas*, 50).
29 Studenna-Skrukwa, *Ukrains'kyi Donbas*, 232.
30 Kuromiya, *Freedom and Terror in the Donbas*, 53–54.
31 Ibid, 53.
32 Quoted in Louise McReynolds, *The News under Russia's Old Regime: The Development of a Mass-Circulation Press* (Princeton, NJ: Princeton University Press, 1991), 110–111.
33 Studenna-Skrukwa, *Ukrains'kyi Donbas*, 233.

Ambivalent Euroscepticism

The European history of Donbas could easily have become an alternativ
to the Soviet image of the "land of miners and metallurgists," or at least a
"landmark" to attract tourists. But the official Soviet historiography erased a
links between the region and Europe (it is no coincidence that in 1924 Yuzivka
was renamed Stalino), and any scholars who took an interest in these issues
were persecuted.[34] During the independence era, local authorities were similarly
reluctant to refer to "European roots," because their priority was promoting ties
with Russia.

As a result, the European heritage of Donbas is currently receiving more
attention from interested researchers and former colonizing countries than from
the local population or local or central government. Ukrainian artist Roman
Minin, a painter, graphic artist, and photographer born in the town of Dymytriv
(renamed Myrnohrad in 2016) in the Donetsk region, said in an interview for
Oleksandr Mykhed's book *I'll Mix Your Blood with Coal: Snapshots from the East
of Ukraine* that he did not learn about John Hughes until he was an adult.[35] In
focus groups on attitudes toward the European Union conducted in 2020 in six
cities in Ukrainian-controlled areas of Donetsk and Luhansk regions, none of
the participants mentioned the area's European heritage.[36] Since independence,
the region has become associated with strong anti-European and anti-NATO
sentiments, which have been confirmed by opinion polls.

Anyone trying to explain the causes and sources of "Euroscepticism" in
Donetsk and Luhansk before 2014 faces the following challenges: first, the lack
of previous studies that would explain rather than just claim such sentiments
among the population; and second, the lack of sociological surveys focusing
on the Donetsk and Luhansk regions[37] rather than the "East" as a macro-region
(which in some surveys could encompass only the Kharkiv, Donetsk, and

---

34 Mykhailo Bublyk, "Lysychans'k. Ievropeis'ka istoriia Donbasu" [Lysychansk. A European
history of Donbas], Ukrinform, March 3, 2018, https://www.ukrinform.ua/rubric-
regions/2415024-lisicansk-evropejska-istoria-donbasu.html.

35 Roman Minin, "The Main Point of Pride of the Residents of the Donetsk Region Is Their
Ability to Survive," in Mykhed, *I'll Mix Your Blood with Coal*, 154.

36 Kateryna Zarembo, "Ievropeiskyi Donbas: Iak komunikuvaty ievropeis'ku intehraciiu na
Donechchyni ta Luhanshchyni" [European Donbas: How to communicate European integration in the Donetsk and Luhansk regions], Tsentr "Nova Ievropa," 2020, http://library.fes.de/
pdf-files/bueros/ukraine/16646.pdf

37 A notable exception is the "Lviv—Donetsk" research mentioned in Chapter 2.

Luhansk regions, while in others it would also include the Zaporizhzhia region, Sumy region, etc.).

Anti-European and anti-NATO sentiments in the region should be neither equated nor absolutized.

Generally for Ukraine, the choice between integration with Russia or the European Union emerged on a serious political level not in 1991, with the restoration of independence, but in 1998, when then-President of Ukraine Leonid Kuchma issued a decree "On Approving the Strategy of Ukraine's Integration into the EU." Since then, public preferences regarding foreign policy integration have been regularly recorded in opinion polls. Analyzing this data, we note several important trends to put the Euroscepticism of the Ukrainian East in the overall context.

First, the idea of joining a union with Russia (which in different years and in different polls could be called the "Union of Russia and Belarus," "Eurasian Economic Union," "Customs Union," etc.) was quite popular not only in the East but throughout Ukraine—until 2012, it was supported by the absolute (!) majority of the population. Additionally, in terms of public support (as shown in Table 3), it rivaled the idea of integration with the EU (the high level of support for integration with both associations indicates that Ukrainians did not perceive these two projects as mutually exclusive).

Table 3. What is your attitude to . . . (percentage of answers "rather positive"[38])

	2000	2002	2004	2006	2008	2010	2012	2013	2014	2015
. . . the idea of Ukraine joining the Union of Russia and Belarus	40.8	57.8	62.8	61.0	60.2	61.4	56.3	48.9	24.6	21.6
. . . the idea of Ukraine joining the European Union	56.0	44.4	47.9	43.0	44.1	45.5	45.9	41.6	50.9	55.8

---

38 Valerii Vorona, ed., *Ukrain'ske suspil'stvo: Monitoryng sotsial'nykh zmin* [Ukrainian society: Monitoring social changes], issue 6 (20) (Kyiv: Instytut sotsiologii Natsional'noi akademii nauk Ukrainy, 2018), 430.

Moreover, if the question about attitudes toward integration projects was formulated as mutually exclusive alternatives, the difference between support for the two projects narrowed even further. In 2012, when there was one of the lowest levels of support for EU accession in the history of surveys on this issue (almost forty percent of the population), one-third of those surveyed supported joining the Customs Union of Russia, Belarus, and Kazakhstan, and another third did not support either integration vector or were not sure.

Table 4. Which integration direction should Ukraine take? (*Please select one answer*)[39]

	October 2011	February 2012	December 2012	May 2013	March 2014	May 2014
Joining the EU	43.7	38.6	42.4	41.7	45.3	50.5
Joining the Customs Union of Russia, Belarus, and Kazakhstan	30.5	29.7	32.1	31.0	21.6	21.4
Neither joining the EU nor the Customs Union	9.3	11.7	10.5	13.5	19.6	17.4
Not sure	16.4	20.0	15.0	13.7	13.4	10.6

According to other opinion polls (in which the questions were phrased somewhat differently), the level of support for a union with Russia may have been higher and exceeded the level of support for joining the EU. In 2011, the Kyiv International Institute of Sociology provided the following data:

---

39 *Stavlennia gromadian do zovnishn'opolitychnoho vektoru Ukrainy: Rehional'nyi rozriz* [Attitudes of citizens to the foreign policy vector of Ukraine: regional breakdown], Fond "Demokratychni initiatyvy" im. Il'ka Kucheriva, July 31, 2014, https://dif.org.ua/article/stavlennya-gromadyan-do-zovnishnopolitichnogo-vektoru-ukraini-regionalniy-rozriz.

Table 5. This chart presents the main points of view on how Ukraine should develop. Please read them and indicate which point of view you think is more valid than the others.[40]

	Ukraine overall	Breakdown by region			
		West	Center	South	East
Ukraine should strive to join the European Union	33%	63%	40%	20%	9%
Ukraine should strive to cooperate with Russia and join the Single Economic Space with Russia, Belarus, Kazakhstan, and other countries	45%	12%	36%	62%	73%
Ukraine's future lies in preserving its full independence and sovereignty, in making independent political and economic decisions, without joining the EU or SES	13%	18%	14%	11%	11%
Difficult to say	8%	6%	10%	6%	7%

In the East, support for the Union with Russia has indeed been consistently and significantly higher than the national average. According to the Democratic Initiatives Foundation, in May 2013, 40.9% of the population in the Eastern regions supported joining the Customs Union of Russia, Belarus, and Kazakhstan, while 28.6% supported joining the EU. In Donbas, the number of Customs Union supporters was even higher, at 61.8%, while only 11.6% of those surveyed were in favor of joining the European Union.[41]

And yet it would not be entirely fair to claim that people in the Ukrainian East were anti-Europe. Rather, they viewed Europe as something unknown and somewhat suspicious. According to polls, 80% of residents of the Southeast have never been abroad,[42] and the same polls show that people's support for European

---

40 *Stavlennia hromadian do intehratsiinykh proektiv* [Attitudes of citizens to integration projects], Kyivs'kyi mizhnarodnyi instytut sotsiolohii, December 8, 2011, http://kiis.com.ua/img/pr_img/20111208_EU_Z/EU.pdf.

41 *Stavlennia gromadian do zovnishn'opolitychnoho vektoru Ukrainy.*

42 "Mezhi svidomosti. Try chverti ukraintsiv nikoly ne pokydaly kordoniv bat'kivshchyny" [The limits of worldview: Three-quarters of Ukrainians have never traveled beyond their homeland], *Korrespondent*, June 6, 2012, https://ua.korrespondent.net/journal/1357147-korrespondent-mezhi-svidomosti-tri-chverti-ukrayinciv-nikoli-ne-pokidali-kordoniv-batkivshchini.

integration correlated with them having had the chance to see Europe with their own eyes: among those who had never been to the EU, the United States, or Canada, only 45% supported European integration in 2012, while among those who had traveled to these countries, the figure was as high as 79%.[43]

At the same time, "Europe" was present in Donbas as a "simulacrum," a surrogate and/or a preferred destination for emigration. In her book, *Amor[t]e*, Oleksandra Ivaniuk portrays a wealthy Donetsk family that despises everything Ukrainian and does not accept the Euromaidan, but their young daughter persists in learning Italian so that she can marry an Italian and emigrate. After all, Donetsk's luxury venues, such as the Donbas Palace Hotel, the Donetsk City shopping mall, and the La Terazza and Di Vino restaurants, adopted "Western," Latinized names associated with wealth and prestige, rather than being called, for example, "Dvorets Donbas" or "Gorodok" (although it should be mentioned that among the city's elite venues was a restaurant called Пушкинъ, or Pushkin, in the old Imperial Russian spelling). As Olena Stiazhkina said of Donetsk in her book *In God's Language*, the city created a kind of pseudo-Europe within its limits, a Europe as a simulacrum, which it did not want to join but was eager to access: "The city was made to look like a tourist had come back home and started putting up fridge magnets left, right, and center. Half a street looked like Paris and the other half like Marmaris, and over there, in an out-of-the-way spot near the Polytechnic University dormitories, Liverpool and the Beatles monument suddenly emerged, while slightly further away, on the other side of the intersection, a building called Gaudi arose."[44]

Secondly, there was a clear "generation gap" in Donbas in terms of attitudes toward European integration: the Democratic Initiatives Foundation and the Ukrainian Sociology Service found in 2011[45] that young people in Donbas and Crimea (aged 18–29) supported Ukraine's membership in the EU on a par with their peers in other regions of Ukraine: 51% were in favor and only 22% were against.[46]

With regard to attitudes toward NATO, the situation was somewhat more complicated. Until 2014, support for Ukraine joining NATO averaged 15–20%

---

43 Ibid.

44 Olena Stiazhkina, *Movoiu Boha* [In God's language] (Kyiv: Dukh i Litera, 2016), 106.

45 Earlier studies revealed a similar trend, for example, Vira Kovtykha, "Zdorova orientatsiia. Molod'—za vstup do IeS ta NATO" [A healthy orientation. Young people support joining the EU and NATO], *Den'*, June 24, 2004, https://day.kyiv.ua/uk/article/panorama-dnya/zdorova-oriientaciya.

46 *Molodi liudy usikh reh ioniv odnakovo bachat' perevahy vstupu Ukrainy v IeS* [Young people from all regions share the same opinion on the benefits of Ukraine's accession to the EU], Fond "Demokratychni initsiatyvy" im. Il'ka Kucheriva, 2011, https://www.irf.ua/files/ukr/programs/euro/eu_poll_ukr.pdf.

across the country (Table 6), but in the Donetsk region, in 2006, only 2.1% of those surveyed were in favor of the idea (Figure 1).

Table 6. What is your opinion of Ukraine joining NATO? (%)[47]

	2000	2002	2004	2006	2008	2010	2012	2013	2014	2015
Rather negative	33.5	37.9	38.5	64.6	57.7	53.3	54.4	54.4	34.8	34.2
Not sure	41.5	42.6	42.0	22.8	24.1	30.8	29.8	30.8	29.7	21.7
Rather positive	24.9	18.8	18.8	12.7	18.0	15.7	15.3	14.4	34.9	43.0
Did not answer	0.1	0.6	0.7	0.1	0.2	0.3	0.4	0.3	0.6	0.9

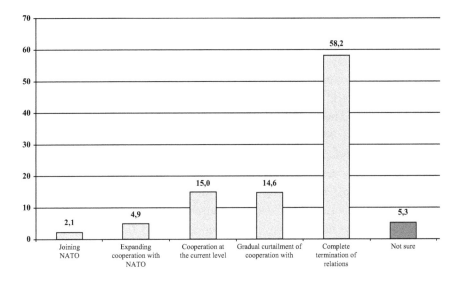

Figure 1.[48] What should Ukraine's policy be on cooperation with NATO at this stage?

---

47 Vorona, *Ukrain'ske suspil'stvo*, 430.
48 Volodymyr Kipen', Ihor Todorov, "Stavlennia do NATO ta inshi zovnishn'opolitychni prio-rytety naselennia Donechchyny" [Attitudes toward NATO and other foreign policy priorities of the population of the Donetsk region], *Visnyk Naukovo-informatsiinoho tsentru mizhnarodnoi bezpeky ta ievroatlantychnoi spivpratsi Donets'koho natsional'noho universytetu* 2 (2005): 30. The "Donetsk region—January 2006" survey was conducted by the Donetsk Institute for Social Research and Political Analysis. The field stage of the survey was conducted from January 20 to January 31, 2006. A total of 1,107 respondents were interviewed in 27 settlements in the Donetsk region—12 towns and 15 villages. The survey was conducted using multistage sampling. The sample is representative of the population of the region in terms of gender, age, education, and type of settlement.

While the European Union evoked mostly positive associations (think of the famous term 'Euroremont,' or Western-style renovation, which indicated relatively high (or higher than usual) quality standards, for example), there were no such commonplace associations with NATO; instead, in the south and east of Ukraine, there was a widespread perception of NATO as an aggressive bloc that, in the minds of those raised with the Soviet mentality, was seen as an enemy rather than an ally.

And yet even in this case, young people held a different opinion. It was on the initiative of young people that pro-European and Euro-Atlantic integration ideas emerged, which materialized into two organizations, the Euroclub and the Center for International Security and Euro-Atlantic Integration. Both of these organizations originated in Donetsk, and the next story in this chapter is about them.

NATO and EU in Donetsk

When Valeriy Kravchenko, then a third-year student at Donetsk University, returned from a summer school in Kyiv on Euro-Atlantic integration in the summer of 2005, he decided to do a project with NATO. He was supported by his academic advisor and other university professors, Ihor Todorov and Yuriy Temirov. They sent off their application to the NATO Information and Documentation Center, and Kravchenko recalled receiving the following response: "We have been waiting for something like this from Donbas for a long time."

The initial project eventually evolved into the Research and Information Center, which was established with the consent and support of the university's rector, Volodymyr Shevchenko, and existed until 2013 (in 2009, an NGO of the same name was also founded). With the support of the NATO Information and Documentation Center, the Center for International Security became the main Euro-Atlantic center in the region: it held what were known as NATO Academies for young people from all over Ukraine and organized informative events, internships, and trips to the Alliance's Headquarters for university students, and its events were attended by Western ambassadors and experts.

At the same time, the center's staff, while personally supporting Ukraine's Euro-Atlantic integration, decided from the outset that their goal was not to campaign among the population, but to inform students, young people, and academics and to bring proactive people together:[49] for many students,

---

49 Valerii Kravchenko, "Ukraina–NATO: vremia real'nogo sblizheniia" [Ukraine–NATO: Time for a closer relationship], *Visnyk Naukovo-informatsiinoho tsentru mizhnarodnoi bezpeky ta ievroatlantychnoi spivpratsi Donets'koho natsional'noho universytetu* 1 (2006): 20.

cooperation with the center was perhaps the first "window into Europe" they had encountered in their lives. Regarding political issues, the center declared its political independence and nonalignment with any political parties and maintained a balanced stance in communicating about cooperation with the Alliance. For example, the center held events on Ukraine-Russia relations in the context of cooperation with the Alliance, invited Russian experts to speak at its public events,[50] and published articles on both the advantages and disadvantages of Ukraine's membership in the Alliance in the *Center for International Security Bulletin*.[51]

The center's representatives did not hide their commitment to the Alliance and to Ukraine's Euro-Atlantic integration (after all, in 2007, the center's deputy head, Ihor Todorov, had defended his doctoral dissertation "European and Euro-Atlantic Integration of Ukraine: National and Regional Dimensions (1991–2004)" at the Donetsk University, and not a single member of the academic council voted against it!), but they also sometimes presented it in subtle ways: among other things, in 2007, the center organized a university soccer team whose emblem was a NATO aircraft.[52] The team was called AWACS, which stands for Airborne Warning & Control System, or, as it is also popularly called, "NATO's eyes in the sky."[53] The center hoped that, for the initiated, the name would imply a connection with the Alliance, but at the same time it would not provoke a negative reaction from the general public.

From today's perspective, it may seem that the local authorities should have interfered with the center's work. And yet the stance taken by local representatives of the Party of Regions was moderate: after all, in 2006–2007, Viktor Yanukovych even served as a prime minister under the presidency of Viktor Yushchenko, whose program included Ukraine's European and Euro-Atlantic integration. Anti-NATO campaigns in the Donetsk region were stirred up

---

50 "Materialy mizhnarodnoi naukovoi konferentsii 'Vidnosyny Ukraina-NATO ta Rosiia-NATO u novykh realiiakh mizhnarodnoi bezpeky,' Donets'k, 24–26 travnia 2009 r." [Proceedings of the International Research Conference "Ukraine–NATO and Russia–NATO Relations in the New Realities of International Security," Donetsk, May 24–26, 2009], *Visnyk Naukovo-informatsiinoho tsentru mizhnarodnoi bezpeky ta ievroatlantychnoi spivpratsi Donets'koho natsional'noho universytetu* 1–2 (2009): 11–59. It is worth noting that this type of "broad dialogue" was generally characteristic of the work being done by independent NGOs of that time that promoted European and Euro-Atlantic integration.

51 Oleksandr Krapivin, "Metodychni rekomendatsii dlia lektoriv, studentiv, aspirantiv ta vykladachiv" [Methodical recommendations for lecturers, undergraduate students, postgraduate students, and faculty], *Visnyk Naukovo-informatsiinoho tsentru mizhnarodnoi bezpeky ta ievroatlantychnoi spivpratsi Donets'koho natsional'noho universytetu* 2 (2007): 5–9.

52 "F.C. Awacs," Facebook, https://www.facebook.com/fcAwacs.

53 "AWACS: NATO's 'eyes in the sky,'" North Atlantic Treaty Organization, March 3, 2022, https://www.nato.int/cps/en/natohq/topics_48904.htm.

primarily by Natalia Vitrenko's Progressive Socialist Party of Ukraine and local representatives of the Communist Party. A story from 2006 is especially telling: a faction of Vitrenko's party proposed to the Donetsk Regional Council that the region should be declared "NATO-free territory."[54] During the vote on whether to put this issue on the meeting's agenda, only 17 members of the Regional Council voted in favor, while 90 voted against.[55] In 2010, representatives of Vitrenko's party even disrupted an international conference being held at Donetsk National University, "NATO–Ukraine, NATO–Russia Relations in the Context of NATO's New Strategic Concept," accusing Viktor Yanukovych of issuing instructions to organize "propaganda work that would shape public opinion with the aim of drawing Ukraine into NATO."[56]

After 2010, the center's work underwent changes. Yet the reason for this was not so much the change of government in Kyiv as the change in rector at the university: with the new administration, holding events at the university became much more difficult. The Center therefore switched to the kind of neutral city venues typically used by NGOs: hotel conference rooms and press centers. Furthermore, center representatives noted that after the change of central government, in some ways it became even easier to continue their work: the updated Law on the Fundamentals of Domestic and Foreign Policy included a clause on "non-alignment," Ukraine's integration into NATO as a political goal disappeared from the agenda, while cooperation with the Alliance remained at the same level: the Annual National Ukraine–NATO Program was being implemented, Ukraine continued participating in NATO exercises and receiving assistance from the Alliance, etc. Thus, the "non-alignment" clause eliminated the need for anti-propaganda that may have hindered the center's work in previous years. In 2013, Valeriy Kravchenko even gave talks on Ukraine–NATO cooperation for representatives of local authorities, district and city councils in the Donetsk region.[57] But by the spring of 2014, it was no longer possible to

---

54 "Sessiia Donetskogo oblsoveta otkazalas' vnosit' v povestku dnia vopros po NATO" [Donetsk Regional Council refuses to put NATO issue on agenda], Kramatorsk.Info, June 5, 2006, https://www.kramatorsk.info/view/16534.

55 Following the 2006 local elections, 120 of the 150 members of the Regional Council were from the Party of Regions.

56 "Boitsy Vitrenko spasli Ianukovicha ot svin'i i sorvali konferentsiiu po NATO v Donetske" [Vitrenko's fighters save Yanukovych from a pig and disrupt NATO conference in Donetsk], *Ostrov*, https://www.ostro.org/news/article-102493/.

57 "Vidnosyny Ukraina—NATO; suchasnyi stan ta perspektyvy" [NATO–Ukraine Relations: Current Status and Prospects], lecture for the secretaries of Donetsk District Councils and City Councils of the Donetsk Region, April 22, 2013, Donetsk, Ukraine. Based on materials of the *Visnyk Naukovo-informatsiinoho tsentru mizhnarodnoi bezpeky ta ievroatlantychnoi spivpratsi Donets'koho natsional'noho universytetu* 1–2 (2013).

hold another NATO Academy in Donetsk, and the event had to be relocated to Ivano-Frankivsk.

The story of the Donetsk Euroclub is somewhat similar to its Euro-Atlantic counterpart. The Euroclub was founded in 2004 on the basis of the Donetsk Institute of the Interregional Academy of Personnel Management, and a year later it became part of Donetsk National University. In 2004, when the Donetsk Institute was just developing its European Studies program, the faculty observed that students were interested not only in theory but also in informal communication, practical activities, etc. This was the impetus for the founding of the Euroclub.

As with the Center for International Security, the Euroclub did not aim to promote Ukraine's European choice politically; its goal was a combination of awareness-raising and volunteer work, and organizing trips to the European Union for students under the Youth in Action program. For many members of the community, the Euroclub's work was not so much about Ukraine's European integration at the national or local level as about personal develop-ment: they learned about what international organizations do, improved their organizational and leadership skills, and had the opportunity to travel. In 2005, the Euroclub, the Center for International Security, and a number of other educational and non-government organizations in Donetsk working in the area of Ukraine's European integration formed the "European Donbas" Coalition.[58] Its purpose was simple: to deepen cooperation and networking among the coa-lition's members. However, what is significant about this story is that as far back as 2005, there were already at least seventeen organizations (coalition members) in Donetsk that considered themselves engaged in the European integration of the region and the country.

Core members of the Euroclub participated in the work on European integra-tion in other formats as well: Serhiy Shtukaryn, for example, sat on the Public Expert Council at the Ukrainian section of the EU–Ukraine Cooperation Committee, which was formed in 2008 as a joint initiative by Hryhoriy Nemyria, the Deputy Prime Minister for European and International Integration (and incidentally, also a native of Donetsk; he wrote the introduction to the Ukrainian edition of Hiroaki Kuromiya's *Freedom and Terror in the Donbas*), and representatives of NGOs.

---

58 "Uhoda pro hromads'ku koalitsiiu v sferi ievropeis'koi ta ievroatlantychnoi intehratsii 'Donbas Ievropeis'ky i'" [Agreement on the "European Donbas" coalition for European and Euro-Atlantic integration], *Visnyk Naukovo-informatsiinoho tsentru mizhnarodnoi bezpeky ta ievroatlantychnoi spivpratsi Donets'koho natsional'noho universytetu* 2 (2006): 3–8.

Unlike Euro-Atlantic integration, Ukraine's European integration had never been questioned by the Party of Regions until the Euromaidan events: it is worth mentioning that it was during Viktor Yanukovych's presidency that the negotiations on the EU-Ukraine Association Agreement were completed. Until the end of 2013, the local authorities not only did not block the work of the university's pro-European centers: they supported it, sending their representatives to Days of Europe, international roundtables on European integration, and so on. With the backing of Jan Tombiński, the then Head of the EU Delegation to Ukraine, an EU Information Center was opened at Donetsk National University in May 2013.[59] But during the Euromaidan, the attitude toward the Euroclub changed dramatically: according to the recollections of participants involved in the events, the governor summoned the then-rector for a meeting, after which the Euroclub was deprived of its premises in the university. The EU flag was one of the first things to leave the building—it ended up at the Euromaidan in Donetsk.

Like most of the people featured in this book, the center's representatives were forced to leave in 2014. Valeriy Kravchenko and Andriy Karakuts live in Kyiv and continue the work of the Center for International Security as an NGO. Ihor Todorov moved to Uzhhorod and at the time of writing is a professor at Uzhhorod National University and director of the university's Center for International Security and Euro-Atlantic Integration.

The Euromaidans of Ukraine's East

Just like the Kyiv Euromaidan, the Donetsk Euromaidan began with a Facebook post on November 22, 2013. Only instead of Mustafa Nayyem, it was Donetsk's Yevhen Nasadyuk (who also wrote under the pseudonym Piotr Armianovski), a local playwright and director:

> I'm getting on my bike to go to the Shevchenko monument. I support the development of Ukraine, the implementation of laws, fair courts, accountability of the authorities to the people, respect for each other, against corruption—all the things we call European values.[60]

---

59 "Informatsiinyi Tsentr IeS" [EU Information Center], Donets'kyi natsional'nyi universytet imeni Vasylia Stusa, https://www.donnu.edu.ua/uk/informatsiyniy-tsentr-yes/.

60 Quoted in *Ievromaidan u Donets'ku. Istoriia borot'by za hidnist'* [Euromaidan in Donetsk. The story of the fight for dignity] (Lviv: PAIS, 2021), 3.

Five people came to Donetsk's Euromaidan that evening: Yevhen Nasadyuk, Kateryna Zhemchuzhnykova, a journalist from the Donetsk Region Apolitical News Portal, Maksym Kasyanov, a journalist, and two other local residents. The following day, Kateryna wrote a news story about the beginning of the Euromaidan in Donetsk. She was criticized for calling a gathering of five people a rally, to which she replied, "This is not about numbers: it's about unity."

Initially, the Donetsk Euromaidan remained relatively small: in the first few weeks, 200–300 people gathered in the square.[61] And yet those who took part in the events are convinced that the number of Euromaidan supporters in Donetsk was actually much higher. This was confirmed by opinion polls: approximately twenty percent of the population of Donbas did support the Euromaidan (which is significantly more than the number of people who came to the square, and suggests that one in five people indirectly supported the protest).[62]

Why, then, did so few Donetsk residents come out to protest? There are several explanations for this. First, many young people traveled to the Kyiv Maidan, where they could experience being at the epicenter of events and also avoid potential problems at their workplace or university. Secondly, Donetsk still remembered the brutal suppression of peaceful gatherings: not only the participants of the 2004 Orange Revolution, who, in the words of Stanislav Fedorchuk, were "hunted like hares," but also more recent events, such as the 2012 protest by Chornobyl victims against the abolition of their benefits, during which one of the miners was killed by security forces.[63] Third, there was also an AutoMaidan in Donetsk, which was separate from the Euromaidan rallies near the Shevchenko monument.

It is important to emphasize that Euromaidans did not just take place in Donetsk—Euromaidan protests started in Luhansk on November 24 and in Kramatorsk on November 22, and protests also went on in Pokrovsk, Kostiantynivka, Mariupol, and other cities in the Donetsk and Luhansk regions. Some of the protesters, such as students from Mariupol State University, were

61 Kateryna Iakovlenko, "Hudok Akhmetovu, abo zhaduiuchy Donets'kyi maidan" [Akhmetov's whistle, or remembering the Donetsk Maidan], Historians.in.ua, October 17, 2024, https://www.historians.in.ua/index.php/en/avtorska-kolonka/1299-kateryna-yakovlenko-hudok-akhmetovu-abo-zhaduiuchy-donetskyi-maidan.

62 Ella Libanova and Mykola Dmytrenko, "Chomu same Donbas stav mistsem natsional'noi tra-hedii? Poshuk nepolityzovanoi vidpovidi na politychne pytannia" [Why did Donbas become a place of national tragedy? Searching for a non-politicized answer to a political question], *Naukovi zapysky Instytutu politychnykh i etnonatsional'nykh doslidzhen' imeni I. F. Kurasa Natsional'noi akademii nauk Ukrainy* 5–6 (2015): 31.

63 Ukrains'kyi instytut natsional'noi pam'iati, Usnyi arkhiv [Ukrainian institute of national memory, Oral history archive], interview with Stanislav Fedorchuk.

outraged by the hypocrisy of the authorities, who had been assuring them of the importance of European integration for years, only to change course overnight.[64]

The Donetsk and Luhansk Euromaidans also organized cultural events, similar to those that took place on the Maidan in Kyiv. In both Donetsk and Luhansk, there was a yellow and blue piano (in Luhansk it was called the "Instrument of Freedom"[65]) that anyone could play. In Donetsk, there were concerts by Serhiy Zhadan and his rock band, Sobaky v kosmosi (Dogs in Space), and the Haidamaky band, while at Euromaidans in the Donetsk and Luhansk regions, Christmas *verteps* put on performances and public intellectuals gave talks (well-known historian and journalist Vakhtang Kipiani came to the Donetsk Euromaidan).[66] Additionally, the Donetsk Euromaidan received support from other regions: Lviv activists helped out with equipment for concerts, while Ternopil provided information leaflets.[67]

The Euromaidans in the East had staunch ideological opponents (Anti-Maidan supporters also accounted for about twenty percent of the population[68]). In Luhansk, for example, there was the so-called Luhansk Guard. According to Luhansk human rights activist Kostiantyn Reutskyi, it was even possible to find common ground with them, as their demands mostly coincided with those of the Euromaidan: "They also wanted justice, accountability of the authorities, transparent relations with the authorities, oversight and decentralization."[69] Yet it was not them who posed the real threat to the protesters.

It is remarkable that even these few hundred active citizens, who numerically could not possibly have posed any threat to the local authorities, were subjected to pressure and physical attacks. There was also evidence that as early as December 2013, police were patrolling the center of Donetsk, stopping anyone who seemed to them to be potential protesters and sending them home, and students were being threatened with expulsion for missing classes.[70] In December 2013, it took activists in Luhansk three attempts before they were

64 Mykhailo Shtekel', Iryna Horbas'ova, "Smel'chaki. Kakim byl Maidan v gorodakh Donbassa" [Daredevils: What was the Maidan like in the cities of Donbas?], Radio Svoboda, November 21, 2017, https://www.radiosvoboda.org/a/donbass-realii/28868187.html.

65 Ukrains'kyi instytut natsional'noi pam'iati, Usnyi arkhiv, interview with Kostiantyn Reutskyi.

66 *Ievromaidan u Donets'ku*, 8–10.

67 Ibid., 6.

68 Libanova and Dmytrenko, "Chomu same Donbas stav mistsem natsional'noyi trahedii?," 31.

69 Ukrains'kyi instytut natsional'noi pam'iati, Usnyi arkhiv, interview with Kostiantyn Reutskyi.

70 Andrii Vyshyns'kyi, "Patruli, revviiskrada i 'smotriashchi'. Donets'k chasiv Ievromaidanu" [Patrols, Revolutionary Military Council, and 'point men.' Donetsk during the Euromaidan], *Ekonomichna pravda*, December 16, 2013, https://www.epravda.com.ua/columns/2013/12/16/408879/.

able to hold a public screening of the documentary *Mezhyhirya*[71] about the life of Viktor Yanukovych: the first screening was drowned out,[72] and during the second screening the equipment was damaged. The third time, the screening did take place, although there were attempts to disrupt it with firecrackers and smoke grenades.[73] In late December 2013, farmers from the Mariinka district, led by Vitaliy Pozhydayev, were summoned for questioning by the Donetsk regional tax administration because they had transferred their Association of Farmers membership fees to the Kyiv Euromaidan.[74]

In January 2014, the situation for Euromaidan participants in Donetsk began to deteriorate. Local TV channels portrayed the Euromaidan protesters as extremists who wanted to overthrow Viktor Yanukovych.[75] Donetsk Euromaidan activists recall that people began receiving threatening messages on their phones and social media—and not only those who came to the Maidan, but even people who were not even in the city at the time.[76] Later, posters with threats, containing photos of protesters and their addresses and passport details, were plastered on houses.[77]

Along with psychological pressure, acts of physical violence began to take place. January 19, 2014 saw the arrival in Donetsk of the *titushky*—representatives of boxing clubs in Horlivka led by Armen Sarkisian (Armen Horlivskyi), a criminal gang leader associated with Yuriy Ivanyushchenko, an influential MP

---

71 Viktor Yanukovych's lavish former mansion and estate outside Kyiv, now a museum of corruption (translator's note).

72 It is worth noting that "noise terror" has been used as a method of preventing dissent since Soviet times: in Luhansk there were attempts to drown out the Euromaidan by Did Moroz singing from a nearby stage at full volume ("Luhan'skyi Maidan: Istoriia sprotyvu z elementamy istorii kokhannia" [The Luhansk Maidan: The story of resistance with elements of the story of love], Natsional'nyi muzei Revoliutsii Hidnosti, https://www.maidanmuseum.org/uk/node/1076), and in 1989, when meetings of pro-Ukrainian activists were held, almost every lawnmower in the city would be taken there (according to Pavlo Zhovnirenko's memoirs in Bilets'kyi et al., *My ydemo!*

73 Ukrains'kyi instytut natsional'noi pam'iati, Usnyi arkhiv, interview with Kostiantyn Reutskyi.

74 *Ievromaidan u Donets'ku*, 26.

75 "Donets'komu Ievromaidanu—6 rokiv: Iak tse bulo ta shcho chekaie na Donbas—rozpoviaiut' uchasnyky podii" [The sixth anniversary of the Donetsk Euromaidan: participants in the events tell the story of what happened and share their thoughts on what the future holds for Donbas], *Ukrains'ke radio*, November 21, 2019, http://www.nrcu.gov.ua/news.html?newsID=91750.

76 Iakovlenko, "Hudok Akhmetovu."

77 Serhii Stukanov and Dmytro Tuzov, "Iak rozpochynavsia i borovsia z rezhymom Ianukovycha donets'kyi Ievromaidan" [How did the Donetsk Euromaidan emerge and fight against the Yanukovych regime?], *Hromads'ke radio*, November 22, 2017, https://hromadske.radio/podcasts/hromadska-hvylya/yak-rozpochynavsya-i-borovsya-z-rezhymom-yanukovycha-doneckyy-yevromaydan.

from the Party of Regions. Tetiana Zarovna, a journalist at *Hazeta po-ukrainsky*, claimed to have evidence that *titushky* had come out of the Donetsk regional administration's building shortly before attacking the activists.[78]

On January 22, 2014, five Euromaidan protesters in Donetsk were attacked and beaten. The activists circulated an appeal to the central authorities accusing the local government—both the regional and city administrations—of complicity and direct responsibility for the attacks on the activists. According to eyewitnesses, the local police had done nothing to prevent the violence, only watched it unfold.[79] But the appeal remained unanswered.

Civil society therefore had no choice but to take over the function of ensuring security. In Kyiv, the Euromaidan self-defense units were made up of different sorts of people, but in Donetsk, it was the Donetsk ultras—Shakhtar FC fans— who ensured the safety of the peaceful protesters.

Moreover, the vast majority of residents of the region did not support either the Maidan or the Anti-Maidan, which could be attributed to opposition to the slogans with which the protesters rallied, and their opposition to such protests in general.[80]

It is worth noting that the lack of support in the East for European integration (in the sense of joining the European Union) could be explained not by a negative view of Europe as such, but rather by the "inferiority complex at the national level" which is manifest in the idea that we would start integration only when we could negotiate with Europe as equals. At the end of 2013, BBC Ukraine published examples of the arguments put forward by Euromaidan opponents. One of the respondents in this non-representative survey, a private entrepreneur from the Donetsk region, explained her position as follows.

> Today, I'm against the signing of the Association Agreement
> with the EU for several reasons. For me, what really matters is
> not whether we will be in the EU, but in what capacity. As far as
> I understand, the EU needs us as an accessory and a market for

---

78 Iakovlenko, "Hudok Akhmetovu."

79 Karina Ohanesian, "'Ultras' proty 'titushok': donets'kyi Ievromaidan berut pid zakhyst" ["Ultras" against *titushky*: Donetsk Euromaidan is taken under protection], *Deutsche Welle*, January 24, 2014, https://p.dw.com/p/1AwhB.

80 Stanislav Aseyev, in his book *In Isolation*, offers a revealing comment on this using the example of the absolutized cult of work: "'The Donbas is at work' is the phrase that will answer any question. [. . .] It is the answer even to *the Maidan itself, where people dared to do the unthinkable: to convert working hours not into the number of screws they had drilled but into songs and warm coffee by the heat of a burning fire* [emphasis mine—K.Z.]. That is a foreign language that was never taught—and is that our fault?" Aseyev, *In Isolation*, 49.

their products, and the products we produce cannot compete with European ones.

I'm also concerned about the EU's demand to raise gas and utility prices for the population, while salaries and pensions will remain unchanged. As far as I know, about 30% of Ukrainians can't afford to pay for utilities as it is—without raising tariffs.

The entire Ukrainian economy is tied to the former CIS countries, which provide us with jobs, sales, and budget revenues. If these ties are severed, our factories will shut down and we could go into default.

No one's stopping us from bringing our culture and education up to European standards. Instead of protesting, young people should start studying according to European standards, getting grades for their knowledge, not for bribes. Then our diplomas would be recognized at the same level as European ones.

No one's stopping us from taking care of the environment, protecting our country, and developing, so we can become a sophisticated, intelligent state and then be able to join the EU as equals.

First, we need to sort ourselves out, and the government should stop robbing their citizens blind. We need our laws to apply to everyone, so that everyone is equal, just like in Europe. Because right now, our country is mired in corruption.[81]

These messages about being an "accessory and a market," "the inability of Ukrainian products to compete with European ones," "reforms first, accession later," and "accession as equals" were reiterated in the East in later years. In particular, they were noticed in focus groups run by the Democratic Initiatives Foundation and the New Europe Center in 2018 and 2020, respectively.[82]

The Donetsk Maidan broke out in earnest when the Kyiv Maidan had already begun to fade away, mourning the Heavenly Hundred Heroes and transforming into a volunteer movement to resist Russian aggression. When the "Russian

---

81 "Chy potriben nam IeS: Arh umenty oponentiv Ievromaidanu" [Do we need the EU? Euromaidan opponents put forward their arguments], BBC Ukraine, November 28, 2013, https://www.bbc.com/ukrainian/politics/2013/11/131128_opponents_eu_vc.

82 "Ievroskeptykiv menshaie, ale roboty shche bahato—eksperty" [There are fewer Eurosceptics, but there is still a lot of work to be done, experts say], Hromads'ka synergiia, October 2, 2018, https://www.civic-synergy.org.ua/news/yevroskeptykiv-menshaye-ale-roboty-shhe-bagato-eksperty/.

Spring" came to Donbas—in the form of a massive influx of Russian troops, cliques of radicals, and mercenaries—even those who had not supported the Euromaidan came out to Donetsk's squares. The slogan of the rally which gathered 10,000 people on March 13, 2014 was "For a united and peaceful Ukraine." It was organized by the newly created Committee of Patriotic Forces of Donbas. On the same day, the first Heavenly Hundred hero from Donetsk, twenty-two-year-old Dmytro Cherniavskyi, a spokesman for the Svoboda (Freedom) party, was stabbed to death.[83] Similar rallies in support of a united Ukraine were held after February 20, 2014 in Luhansk.[84]

The protests continued, as did the establishment of the "Donetsk" and "Luhansk" "people's republics." On April 17, Volodymyr Rybak, a member of Horlivka City Council from the Batkivshchyna (Fatherland) party who had attempted to reinstall the Ukrainian flag on the city council building instead of the "DPR" flag, went missing. His body was found a few days later showing signs of torture. Staying in the occupied cities was becoming increasingly dangerous, and in May 2014, many residents of the Donetsk and Luhansk regions were forced to leave their homes. What happened later is a story of occupation that continues to this day and is beyond the scope of this book. The last peaceful campaign, which continued in occupied Donetsk for several more months, was the Prayer Marathon: a small tent was put up in Constitution Square near the Kalmius River where clergy of various denominations simply prayed for Ukraine.

***

As regards the Ukrainian-controlled territories of the Donetsk and Luhansk regions, the narratives slowly changed after 2014. Olena Stiazhkina recalls in an interview for Oleksandr Mykhed's book:

> My colleagues and I traveled through the East, presenting the book *Work, Exhaustion, and Success: Industrial Monocities of Donbas*, and a wonderful story happened to us.
>
> Kostiantynivka was the first city we visited. We had a good, sincere conversation, and towards the end, one person stood up and said: "That's all great, but Kostiantynivka was created by the Belgians. You should write about that!"

83 Mykhailo Zhyrokhov, "Persha vtrata donets'koho Ievromaidanu. Istoriia aktyvista Dmytra Cherniavs'koho" [The first loss of the Donetsk Euromaidan. The story of activist Dmytro Cherniavskyi], *Rubryka*, March 13, 2019, https://rubryka.com/article/dmytro-chernyavskyj/.

84 Ukrains'kyi instytut natsional'noi pam'iati, Usnyi arkhiv, interview with Kostiantyn Reutskyi.

The second city was Druzhkivka. The discussion was excellent: professional, fruitful; other people's reflections were very interesting. At the end, people said: "Yuzivka was created by the English, and you know, English capitalism is very similar to American, it's just as exhausting. But Druzhkivka was created by the French, we had theaters, galleries, horse racing, brothels—well, everything French."

Then we went to Kramatorsk. At the end of our presentation—a more official one this time—one of the listeners asks: "Did you know that Kramatorsk was founded by the Swiss?"

I felt like I'd traveled all over Europe in less than a day, without leaving the Ukrainian East.

On this trip, I saw with my own eyes how one myth—without coercion, without "control from above"—had been replaced by another. And if the war can have any positive consequences, then that's one of them.[85]

***

In August 2021, news surfaced on the internet that the Belgian hospital building in Lysychansk could be given a new life. Supposedly, there were plans to create a new urban space with creative hubs, cinemas, museums, exhibition halls, etc. At least that was the idea announced by the regional administration.[86] Back in 2017, the Metacity: East project team had recognized the European heritage of Lysychansk as among the factors with the greatest potential for bringing social and environmental change to the city.[87]

Since July 2, 2022, Lysychansk has been temporarily occupied by the Russian Federation. The Belgian gymnasium in Lysychansk was destroyed by Russian shelling in May 2022.

***

85 Olena Stiazhkina: "The Gulag Was No Longer Needed. Camps Were Pointless because the Camp Was Embedded within Me," in Mykhed, *I'll Mix Your Blood with Coal*, 275.

86 Nika Bogun, "Mul'tykhab, park ta observatoriia: Shcho planuiut u Lysychans'ku stvoryty na mistsi zruinovanoi bel'hiiskoi likarni" [Multihub, park, and observatory: what is being planned for the site of the ruined Belgian hospital in Lysychansk], V chas pik, August 12, 2021, https://vchaspik.ua/ua/regiony/508539-multyhab-park-ta-observatoriya-shcho-planuyut-u-lysychansku-stvoryty-na-misci.

87 Iryna Iakovchuk, "#urbandoslidzhennia: Indeks shchastia Lysychans'ka" [Urbanresearch: Lysychansk happiness index], *Big Idea*, July 9, 2017, https://biggggidea.com/practices/urbanistichne-doslidzhennya-indeks-schastya-lisichanska/.

May 2021. Sievierodonetsk. Thirty kilometers (just under 20 miles) from the front line. At the invitation of the Center for International Security, I participated as a speaker at the NATO Academy held at the Volodymyr Dahl East Ukrainian National University. None of the foreign experts and diplomats opted to attend in person—off the record, we were making fun of the exaggerated (as it then seemed) anxiety of our Western colleagues.

During Barbora Maronkova's video presentation from NATO Headquarters in Brussels, uniformed men entered the room and asked us to leave—they had received a report that the university building had been rigged with explosives. Bomb squads checked the premises and found nothing. The academy's work was interrupted, but it resumed a few hours later, when the planned events were moved to locations outside the university. Foreign diplomats and academy participants were sure that the timing of the academy and the anonymous bomb alert was not a coincidence.

During the diploma awarding ceremony, some academy participants asked not to be photographed: their families were still in the occupied territories and they did not want to put them at risk.

It was less than a year before Russia's full-scale invasion.

Chapter 5

The Villages of Ukraine's East as Carriers of Ukrainian Markers

———————

Perhaps the most revealing illustration of the marginalization of villages in Donbas is the fact that Google knows almost nothing about them. My searches for "village in Donetsk region," "village in Luhansk region," and "village in Donbas" result in a few links that bring me to the websites of amalgamated territorial communities, the result of the recent decentralization reform. No articles, no news stories, no research.

Olena Stiazhkina was right: the village fell out of—or rather was deliberately excluded from—the Soviet myth.[1] There was no place for the village in the land of miners and metallurgists and the Soviet proletariat, as the Soviet government portrayed it. And yet the village was there, and it was there long before the industrial cities of Donbas appeared (this is where we refute the romantic metaphor of Donbas as a "wild steppe" or "wild fields"—there were fields and steppes, of course, but they were not wild, not if we understand wildness as something completely untouched). The industrial history of the region only dates back to the mid-nineteenth century, while settlements there appeared much earlier and the oldest villages and towns have a history of several hundred years, such as Yasynuvata, founded in 1690 as a Cossack palanka.[2] The ancient Ukrainian

---

1   Stiazhkina, "The Gulag Was No Longer Needed," 267.
2   Oleksandr Palii, "Lyst do brativ-skhidniakiv" [Letter to our brothers from the East], *Ukrains'ka pravda*, August 1, 2007, https://www.pravda.com.ua/articles/2007/08/1/3264555/.

villages that existed before the industrialization of the region—before the area became "Donbas"—can be identified by their names: Mistky, Yamy, Zaporizke, Poltavske, Volodarske, Boyove.[3] In 1897, when the urban population density in Ukraine was 16.1%, it was less than 8% in the Donetsk region and only 4.2% in the Luhansk region.[4] The rest of the population were peasants.

Moreover, by the end of the nineteenth century, a dichotomy of "industrial Russian city vs. Ukrainian village" had already formed in Donbas, representing two different, sometimes mutually antagonistic worlds. According to the 1897 census, cited by Marta Studenna-Skrukwa, 74% of workers in the Donbas mining industry were Russians and 22% Ukrainians. In the metallurgical industry, 69% of the workers were Russian and 22.2% Ukrainian.[5] Meanwhile, 68% of agricultural workers were Ukrainian and only 18.3% were Russian, as is demonstrated in the example of three Donbas counties—Bakhmut, Mariupol, and Slovianoserbsk.[6] Local villagers were reluctant to accept work in the mines, and if they did, they preferred working on the surface.[7] Those Ukrainians who were miners, both locals and newcomers, continued to work on their vegetable patches and raise livestock, while the Russian workers lived in barracks.[8]

The Holodomor—the Soviet-orchestrated famine in the early 1930s—drastically altered the social fabric of the Donetsk and Luhansk regions, wiping the history of many settlements, or even the villages themselves, off the face of the earth, and Russification and Sovietization were less pronounced in the countryside than in the city. It was the villages of the Donetsk and Luhansk regions that remained pockets of the Ukrainian language throughout the Soviet era, in contrast to the Russified cities. It is worth taking a look at the language distribution in the districts of the Donetsk and Luhansk regions as recorded in the 2001 census (the names of the districts are presented in the 2001 version

---

3   This list of towns is taken from Serhiy Zhadan's interview and Oleksandr Paliy's article (cited above). Serhiy Zhadan also offers another example: settlements that emerged from Cossack villages are constructed differently than those built around mines. Source: Serhiy Zhadan: "If We Don't Want the East to Be Separated, We Need to Get to Know It," in Mykhed, *I'll Mix Your Blood with Coal*, 194.

4   Alla Bochkovs'ka and Leonid Rudenko, "Karty Natsional'noho atlasu Ukrainy iak informatsiina baza dlia doslidzhennia chysel'nosti naselennia" [Maps from the national atlas of Ukraine as an information base for the study of population formation], *Ukrains'kyi heohrafichnyi zhurnal* 2 (2014): 8.

5   Studenna-Skrukwa, *Ukrains'kyi Donbas*, 151.

6   Ibid.

7   Ibid, 153.

8   Stiazhkina, "The Gulag Was No Longer Needed," 268. Stiazhkina also mentions that it was thanks to their vegetable patches and livestock that people managed to survive during the Second World War.

before the decommunization law was implemented). In Donetsk itself, 87.8% of the population indicated Russian as their mother tongue and only 11% of the population indicated Ukrainian as their mother tongue, and in Luhansk, these numbers were 85% and 14% respectively,[9] but in most districts (a district was defined as a settlement with a population of no more than 50,000 people) the Ukrainian language was dominant. As can be seen from Tables 7 and 8, in both Donetsk and Luhansk regions, there are more districts with Ukrainian as a predominant language than districts where mostly Russian was used.

Table 7. Distribution of the population by mother tongue, Donetsk region (as a percentage of the total population, excluding cities of regional significance)

District	Indicated as mother tongue	
	Ukrainian	Russian
Amvrosiivka	43.46	55.77
Artemivsk	72.22	26.22
Velyka Novosilka	50.26	47.43
Volnovakha	58.45	40.36
Volodarka	31.14	67.40
Dobropillia	88.61	10.85
Kostiantynivka	69.84	29.41
Krasnoarmiysk	74.06	25.53
Krasnyi Lyman	82.18	16.96
Mariinka	56.52	43.02
Novoazovsk	40.22	59.33
Pershotravneve	22.35	76.63
Oleksandrivka	89.51	9.98
Sloviansk	83.19	15.55
Starobeshiv	17.06	81.78
Telmanove	39.87	57.17
Shakhtarsk	53.36	46.25
Yasynuvata	40.96	58.21

---

9 Data for the Donetsk region is from "19A050501_02_014. Rozpodil naselennia za ridnoiu movoiu, Donets'ka oblast'," Bank danykh Derzhavnoi sluzhby statystyky Ukrainy," bit.ly/3GCnoQ2. Data for the Luhansk region is from "19A050501_02_044. Rozpodil naselennia za ridnoiu movoiu, Luhans'ka oblast'," bit.ly/3tJXrGC. Both are given according to Bank danykh Derzhavnoi sluzhby statystyky Ukrainy [Census Data Bank]—http://database.ukrcensus.gov.ua/.

Table 8. Distribution of the population by mother tongue, Luhansk region (as a percentage of the total population, excluding cities of regional significance)

District	Indicated as mother tongue	
	Ukrainian	Russian
Antratsyt	46.51	53.10
Bilovodsk	84.20	15.56
Bilokurakyne	91.39	8.37
Krasnodon	27.26	72.32
Kreminna	78.73	20.82
Lutuhyne	49.33	49.82
Markivka	93.78	5.80
Milove	73.84	24.12
Novoaydar	45.99	53.61
Novopskov	92.20	7.52
Perevalsk	23.15	76.39
Popasna	64.08	35.60
Svatove	91.84	7.55
Sverdlovsk	56.01	41.29
Slovianoserbsk	38.94	60.40
Stanytsya Luhanska	14.17	85.06
Starobilsk	79.17	20.48
Troyitske	62.76	36.89

The villages, however, have shrunk significantly. By the end of the twentieth century, the share of the urban population in Donbas had reversed compared to the ratio of a century ago: according to the 1989 census, the share of the urban population was 90.3% in the Donetsk region, 86.4% in the Luhansk region, and only 66.9% for Ukraine as a whole.[10]

That is why the villages of Donetsk and Luhansk regions cannot be overlooked. Because it is the villages that offer an insight into a different, and still largely unknown, Donbas.

---

10 Bochkovs'ka and Rudenko, "Karty Natsional'noho atlasu Ukrayiny," 8.

The Halychany of Donbas. Zvanivka

History moves in circles. After 2014, the phrase "internally displaced persons" became firmly rooted in the Ukrainian lexicon. There was no need to specify where these people were coming from.

And yet the phenomenon of resettlement, both voluntary and forced, is part of the identity of Donbas. Hiroaki Kuromiya discusses this in his book *Freedom and Terror in the Donbas*: as early as the nineteenth century, the steppe became a refuge for fleeing serfs, criminals, those subject to political or religious persecution, and those seeking out opportunities to make money.[11] After World War II, Donbas drew people in as the reconstruction of the region offered opportunities.[12]

There were also those who found themselves in Donbas against their own will. For example, after the Second World War, Lemkos and Boikos from western Galicia were forcibly resettled to the Donetsk and Luhansk regions as part of the exchange of territories between Poland and the Soviet Union. These ethnic groups were not only resettled in Donbas: according to reports, 32,000 Ukrainian Boikos from 35 villages were dispersed across four southern regions of the Ukrainian Soviet Socialist Republic (SSR): 25 villages in the Donetsk (then Stalino) region, 10 villages in the Mykolaiv region, 20 villages in the Odesa region, and 5 villages in the Kherson region.[13]

In Donbas, Lemkos were resettled in the Luhansk region and Boikos in the Donetsk region. There is even a Boikivskyi district in the Donetsk region, which before 2016 was called the Telmanove district.

Many Lemko and Boiko villages have been under occupation since 2014: for example, the village of Peremozhne in the Luhansk region, the villages of Kozatske and Oktyabrske in the Donetsk region, etc.[14] The history of deportation, and the story of their lives in independent Ukraine, are told for them by those who remain in Ukrainian-controlled territory.

At the entrance to the village of Zvanivka in the Bakhmut district, there is a chapel dedicated to the Virgin Mary, a common sight in Galician villages.

---

11 Kuromiya, *Freedom and Terror in the Donbas*, 38.

12 Ibid, 339. Kuromiya notes that between 1945 and 1959, the population of the Stalino region more than doubled, from nearly two million to over four million.

13 Iuliia Chebrets', "Deportovani nazavzhdy. Lemky ta boiky: Khto taki ta iak opynylysia na Skhodi" [Deported forever. Lemkos and Boikos: Who they are and how they ended up in the East], *Hromada Skhid* 19 (October 2020), https://gromadaskhid.com.ua/deportovani-nazavzhdy-hto-taki-bojky-ta-lemky-i-yak-opynylysya-na-shodi/.

14 Ibid.

The streets are clean and decorated with flowers. A red and black Ukrainian Insurgent Army flag is flying on the central building.

Zvanivka, Verkhnokamianske, and Rozdolivka are three villages to which nearly 340 families from the village of Liskowate in western Galicia (until 1951, in Drohobych region, now part of Poland) were deported in 1951. Due to the close proximity of the villages (10–15 kilometers, or 6–9 miles, away from each other) and the high proportion of displaced people among the population, they were fortunate enough to preserve their identity, language, faith, and traditions.[15] These were the only villages in the Bakhmut district where schools have used Ukrainian as the language of instruction since 1951.[16] During Soviet times, the villagers were married and christened clandestinely, as they refused to use the services of an Orthodox priest. There were two churches in the village: a Greek Catholic church (the first Greek Catholic parish in the Donetsk region in independent Ukraine was registered in Zvanivka) and an Orthodox church of the Moscow Patriarchate. Quite understandably, most of the parishioners are members of the former. Zvanivka is also home to Donbas's only Greek Catholic monastery of the Basilian Fathers of the Heart of Christ.

The Soviet government did everything it could to erase the history of the Donetsk region that existed prior to the Soviet occupation. In 2009, BBC correspondent Marta Shokalo came to the Donetsk region to make one of the first media stories in Ukraine about the Ukrainian Donbas,[17] and one of the places she visited was Zvanivka. In the local cemetery she did not find a single grave older than 1941, even though Zvanivka's history goes back several hundred years.[18]

In Soviet times, talking about deportation was so dangerous that the descendants of displaced people often did not know about their parents' heritage. As Oksana Rasulova, a journalist for the Livyi bereh news outlet, aptly put it, "it's not so much about [individual] memory as it is about collective memory. Its place was first taken by fear, and when the fear was gone, only emptiness

---

15 Ibid.
16 Ibid.
17 Fortunately, these stories are still available. Here they are: Shokalo, "Donbas—shakhtarskyi krai"; eadem, "Sut' Donbasu—svoboda i teror"; eadem, "Zastiina kovbasa i holodomory: 3-ii narys pro Donbas" [The sausage of Stagnation and the famines: The third essay on Donbas], BBC News Ukraine, December 24, 2009, https://www.bbc.com/ukrainian/ukraine/2009/12/091224_donbass_3_sp; eadem, "Donets'k chy Donetsk? Movnyi vybir: Narys 4" [Donets'k or Donetsk? The language choice: Essay 4], BBC News Ukraine, December 26, 2009, https://www.bbc.com/ukrainian/ukraine/2009/12/091226_donbass_4_sp.
18 Shokalo, "Sut' Donbasu—svoboda i teror."

remained."[19] And yet since independence, some descendants of displaced people have done a lot of work to restore the memory of their family history, traditions, and lost homeland. The Tutov family from Rozdolivka wrote a book titled *Boikivshchyna–Donbas. Preserving Memory*, featuring memories of the displaced families.[20] In 2013, the Gorky Library in Luhansk published a local history essay, "Lemkos of the Luhansk Region: Pages from History and Culture."[21]

The Boikos and Lemkos of Donbas have managed not only to preserve their history but also to pass it on. The Tymchak family keeps the tradition of *verteps* alive: since 2011, the Christmas event has evolved into a "Christmas *vertep* for everyone in Donbas" campaign, when the Zvanivka *vertep* began visiting schools and orphanages, and after 2014, ATO soldiers too.[22] Zvanivka preserves other traditions as well: lighting bonfires on Ivana Kupala night, cooking traditional Boiko food, such as a special borshch and cabbage rolls with gravy, etc. It was in Zvanivka, right after the restoration of independence, that young Ihnatiy Volovenko was inspired to become a Greek Catholic priest (see Chapter 6 for more on his story).

The decentralization reform allowed Zvanivka and Verkhnyokamyanske to create the smallest amalgamated territorial community in Ukraine, with villagers holding a demonstration in support of this idea in front of the Donetsk Regional State Administration in Kramatorsk.[23] One of the first steps taken by the new community, which has a total population of approximately three thousand people, was to renovate their House of Culture. To use a poetic metaphor, we can say that a culture that had been oppressed and hidden underground for decades under Soviet rule finally has a home.

---

19 Oksana Rasulova, "Za liniieiu pam'iati. Nashchadky boikiv ta lemkiv Donbasu" [Beyond the line of memory. Descendants of the Boikos and Lemkos of Donbas], LB.ua, January 2, 2021, https://lb.ua/society/2021/01/02/474270_liniieyu_pamyati_nashchadki_boykiv_i.html.

20 You can read more about the book here: https://www.istpravda.com.ua/columns/2022/12/5/162128/.

21 "Lemky na Luhanshchyni: Storinky istorii i kul'tury. Kraieznavchy i narys" [Lemkos in the Luhansk region: Pages from history and culture. A local history essay], Luhans'ka oblasna universal'na naukova biblioteka im. O. M. Gor'kogo. Viddil kraieznavchoi informatsii [A. M. Gorky Luhansk regional universal scientific library, Local history information department], https://lib-lg.com/images/razdely_biblioteki/glavnaya/nauchnye_issledovaniya/lemki_i_staroveri.pdf.

22 Volodymyr Rykhlits'kyi, "Iak lemky i boiky buduiut svoiu hromadu na Donbasi" [How Lemkos and Boikos are building their community in Donbas], *Ukrains'ka pravda*, December 13, 2017, https://life.pravda.com.ua/projects/novi-gromadi/2017/12/13/227905/.

23 Ibid.

The Aeneid on the H20 Highway: Oleksandro-Kalynove

We left for Oleksandro-Kalynove from Bakhmut, a quiet green city. The website of the Donetsk Regional State Administration states that it was in Bakhmut that the first blue and yellow flag in Donbas was raised in 1917. Bakhmut was renamed Artemivsk in 1924, but the city remained the center of Donbas until 1932, when the Soviet government moved the center to Donetsk, claiming that Bakhmut had "overly serious Ukrainian traditions."[24] In 2009, Marta Shokalo came to Artemivsk and found people who cherished the memory of the former name: "Me and others like me, we don't say we're from Artemivsk; we're from Bakhmut," said Volodymyr Berezin, whose father and grandfather were born in Bakhmut. "But no one wants to recognize us here. We are told that Bakhmut never existed."[25] In 2016, by a decree of the Ukrainian parliament, the town with a 500-year-old history reclaimed its name, Bakhmut, and with it, the town's place in public memory.

In the morning, with some time on our hands before we had to leave, we walked from the hotel up to the round plaza of the present-day train station and then to the old train station, a local tourist attraction. On the facade of the Aeneas Bookstore on Borysa Horbatova Street, there were two billboards featuring photos of men. In one of them, a young man wearing an embroidered shirt and camouflage pants was smiling from the sepia-colored photo. The caption read: "Anton Ihorovych Tsedik. Call sign 'Aeneas'. 27 years old. A fighter of the Donbas Battalion. Killed on 29.08.2014 during the Battle for Illovaisk."[26] The second photo was of a dark-haired man with a mustache against the background of a blue sky and a wheat field. The caption read: "Artem Miroshnychenko. Brutally murdered for speaking Ukrainian."[27]

***

We took the H20 highway to get to Oleksandro-Kalynove from Bakhmut. Right before turning off for the village, we passed the Kleban Byk landscape park,

---

24 Shokalo, "Sut' Donbasu—svoboda i terror." According to Olena Stiazhkina, Bakhmut was denied the right to become the center because the city was "too mercantile and unproletarian."
25 Ibid.
26 "Aeneas" was killed during the battle for Illovaisk, along with Yuriy Matushchak and their fellow brothers-in-arms. Like Yuriy, he was also a historian by profession.
27 Artem Miroshnychenko, a volunteer from Bakhmut, was killed in his hometown in 2019. At the time of writing, the investigation against the two detainees was still ongoing. According to an accidental witness of the fight, which was first reported by *Ukrains'kyi tyzhden'* (https://tyzhden.ua/sprava-artema-myroshnychenka-napad-za-movu/) the fight broke out because Miroshnychenko was speaking Ukrainian.

another highlight of the region that debunks the myth of Donbas as a land of mines, waste heaps, and polluted air.

A school bus from Lyman arrived at our destination at the same time as we did. Huddled under umbrellas, the crowd of schoolchildren was cramming itself into the first room of the local museum, which had once been a school. Andriy Taraman, our guide and one of the museum's founders, an ATO veteran, activist, and member of the Illinivka City Council, showed the children various household items, asking them to guess their names and purpose. In other rooms, there were exhibitions on everyday items from Soviet times, the environment, and the Russian-Ukrainian war. Not far from the museum there was an old clay-walled hut with a hallway and two rooms—an ethnographic exhibit similar to those found in the Pyrohiv Museum of Folk Architecture in Kyiv. The third space was a patch of grass between the two buildings, where an old Soviet tractor stood on a pedestal.

This tractor is where it all began. Locals say that the tractor worked on a collective farm from 1934 to 1972. When the machine was no longer needed, it was placed on a pedestal as a provider and community favorite (for which the tractor even got its own name, "Udyk"). But in 2009, the Soviet artifact caught the attention of the district authorities: it was then that a museum of local history was established in Kostiantynivka. The tractor never got its own spot in the city museum and was dismantled for spare parts.

It may be difficult for an outside observer to understand why this Soviet-era exhibit, which might otherwise have ended up in the scrapyard, became the catalyst for the "Maidan" in Oleksandro-Kalynove, if by "Maidan" we understand the awakening of civic consciousness. Residents of Oleksandro-Kalynove were outraged by the district authorities' decision to take the tractor away from the community. At first, they wrote letters of complaint, and when that didn't work, they set up their own NGO called Aeneid. When local officials asked them why they needed the tractor, since they didn't even have their own museum, they replied: "We will have the museum eventually." And they created something that has become one of the main tourist attractions of the region. Our guide, Andriy, recited a poem for the schoolchildren that he wrote for the community to defend their beloved tractor: the text's burlesque form conceals the image of civic activism, awakened in confrontation with the authorities.

The fight for "Udyk" spurred the locals not only to establish the NGO and the museum. Since 2013, on the last weekend before Independence Day, the village has hosted Smolyanskyi Kulish, a festival of Ukrainian culture, featuring a parade of *vyshyvankas* (traditional Ukrainian embroidered shirts), Cossack sports competitions, rides on a local transportation invention called a "velouzvar," and free *kulish*, or millet porridge (needless to say, the event was held exclusively in Ukrainian). The name of the festival is derived from the popular name for the area, Smolyanka, which, according to local residents, was used in the nineteenth century (presumably deriving from the name of the local estate holder, Pan Smolyaninov). Behind the fun facade of the event, there is a historical continuity: locals say old maps show that seven roads used to meet in the village, so the community decided to restore the village's role as the center of the area.

Oleksandro-Kalynove is the cultural heart of the district, and since the decentralization reform, it has further consolidated this role. The village's House of Culture and collection of ethnic and theatrical costumes would be the envy of many art schools in Kyiv. Andriy Taraman said the villagers were outraged when Oleksandro-Kalynove was not designated the center of the community after the decentralization reform, and he even went to the Regional Administration to complain. "You have the culture," they told him, "and where there is culture, there is the center."

It doesn't really matter whether these are actual historical facts or beautiful legends spun just for tourists, akin to Lviv's Coffee Mining Manufacture. For the purposes of this research, what is much more important is that small settlements like Zvanivka and Oleksandro-Kalynove (I can't resist the obvious metaphor of "East and West together"), home to barely a thousand people, refute the myth of Donbas as a land of paternalism, civic indifference, and a mentality of helplessness. Before the Russian aggression, these villages had become models of ingenuity where Ukrainian culture in its various manifestations was being preserved, reproduced, and disseminated. Locals say that prior to the Russian aggression, this place, with its beautiful nature and welcoming people, was particularly popular among Donetsk residents: they not only came to visit but also bought plots of land near the village. The occupation of Donetsk put an end to the flow of tourists to the village and halted the tourist development of the area. Clearly, such villages did not fit into the Soviet and post-Soviet myths about Donbas because they utterly refuted it.

My friend, the children's book author Iryna Ozymok, often says: "No one is too small to change the world for the better." These words perfectly fit the small communities of the Ukrainian East.

***

"But why Aeneid?" I asked Andriy, sitting on a red couch in a local grocery store with a paper cup of coffee. Svitlana, the store owner, made me the coffee.

She is also listening to our conversation, leaning back against the windowsill ("Listening to Andriy is such a joy!").

"Well, we just made a list of possible names and rejected them one by one. Finally, only one remained: Aeneid. It's catchy. It also raises questions. And if it raises questions, it will be memorable."

I take notes, and I think about this amazing Aeneid on the H20 highway, and about "Aeneas," and the flowers for him lying outside the Bakhmut bookstore.

***

As of August 2022, Zvanivka and Oleksandro-Kalynove are free territories and are located ten kilometers from the front line.

Chapter 6

"Go Set a Watchman": Protestants, Orthodox Christians, Greek-Catholic Christians, and Muslims of Ukraine's East

---

From the end of February until November 2014, an interdenominational Prayer Marathon was held first in Constitution Square in Donetsk and then clandestinely. Its slogans were not political: the prayers were "For Peace in Ukraine." And yet representatives of the Ukrainian Orthodox Church of the Moscow Patriarchate did not participate in this Christian marathon. Only the Orthodox Christians of the Kyiv Patriarchate, Protestants, Muslims, Catholics, and Greek Catholics stood in the tent under the Ukrainian flag in Donetsk's Constitution Square. From time to time, Buddhists and Jews would also come up to them. Who were these people, and whom did they represent in this region that has such a complex relationship with religion?

In the USSR in general and in Donbas in particular, religion was not tolerated. During the Soviet regime, religious communities were systematically reduced in size, except during the periods of thaws, and believers of various denominations were severely persecuted. At the same time, Orthodoxy, under the jurisdiction of the Moscow Patriarchate, was the favored denomination of local authorities in independent Ukraine. But this is only part of the story.

Protestants: A Conversion

"In the name of the Father . . . the Son . . . and the Holy Spirit . . . Amen!" Gennadiy Mokhnenko's hoarse voice sounds rough and army-like, as if he were more used to giving military orders than reciting the Lord's Prayer. This is a still from the 2015 film *Crocodile Gennadiy, or Almost Holy*, directed by American filmmaker Steve Hoover, about a Protestant pastor from Mariupol, father of three biological and thirty-two adopted children and teenagers, and founder of the Pilgrim Republic rehabilitation center for drug-addicted children.[1]

Protestantism in the Donetsk and Luhansk regions is special, if only because this was the only area of Ukraine where, in the early 2000s, Protestant communities were the most numerous of all religious denominations—in the Donetsk region, they accounted for sixty percent of all believers, exceeding even the Orthodox Church of the Moscow Patriarchate in number.[2] However, by 2014, their number had declined—according to some observers, the approaches that had worked for the Protestants in the crisis-ridden 1990s ceased to be effective in the more stable 2000s.[3] But even today, Protestant churches remain powerful religious structures in the region: for example, the Kramatorsk Church Council includes twenty-two churches, of which the Orthodox Church of Ukraine, Greek Catholics, and other denominations each represent one community, and the rest are Protestant churches.

It is important to note that the term "Protestants" is an umbrella term that encompasses many horizontal and heterogeneous structures and movements. In the Donetsk and Luhansk regions, the most numerous are the communities of Evangelical Baptists, Pentecostals, Charismatics, and, with a slight numerical margin, Seventh-day Adventists.[4]

There are several reasons for the popularity of Protestant doctrine in eastern Ukraine. Perhaps it is worth starting with the fact that the history of Protestantism in the region begins at its origins—Protestants from Western Europe were the first colonizers of the region during the Russian Empire. Oleh Forostiuk, in his work *Religion in the Luhansk Region,* mentions the founder of the Luhansk Foundry, Charles Gascoigne, and the superintendent of the plant, James Walker, who were Scottish Lutherans; the mining superintendent of the Luhansk plant

---

1 The film was screened in Ukraine during the 2016 DocuDays documentary film festival.

2 Viktor Voinalovych and Nataliia Kochan, *Relihiinyi chynnyk etnopolitychnykh protsesiv na Donbasi: Istoriia i suchasnist'* [The religious factor in ethnopolitical processes in Donbas: History and present] (Kyiv: Instytut politychnykh i etnonatsional'nykh doslidzhen' imeni I. F. Kurasa Natsional'noi akademii nauk Ukrainy, 2014), 201.

3 Kateryna Shapoval, "Protestanty z Donbasu. Protestanty vyiavylysia odniieiu z naibil'sh patriotychnykh sotsial'nykh hrup na okhoplenomu viinoiu skhodi krainy" [Protestants from Donbas. Protestants turned out to be one of the most patriotic social groups in the war-torn east of the country], NV, March 23, 2016, https://nv.ua/ukr/publications/protestanti-z-donbasu-protestanti-vijavilisja-odnijeju-z-najbilsh-patriotichnih-sotsialnih-grup-na-ohoplenomu-vijnoju-shodi-krajini-104809.html.

4 Voinalovych and Kochan, *Relihiinyi chynnyk*, 202.

in 1835–1840 was a German Protestant.[5] As early as 1897, more than 13,400 Protestants lived in the Bakhmut, Slovianoserbsk, and Starobilsk districts.[6]

During Soviet times, Protestants in the Ukrainian East, as well as in the rest of Ukraine, were persecuted. They were victims of repression, and it was not until the 1990s that Protestant communities were able to recover. In addition, the Ukrainian East became a key destination for Western missionaries: Voinalovych and Kochan, citing 1990s data from local authorities, claim that 610–680 people a year came to the Donetsk region from 30–40 countries (for the Luhansk region the researchers give more modest figures), a number that has been steadily decreasing since the 2000s.[7] The missionaries brought not only the teachings of Jesus Christ, but also humanitarian aid, which in itself was attractive to the local population.

There are no studies explaining the phenomenon of the popularity of Protestantism in eastern Ukraine, but conversations with representatives of Protestant churches and religious scholars allow us to put forward several hypotheses. First, Protestant churches offered simple and clear answers to some questions for those who were on a spiritual search but did not find answers and acceptance in the dominant Orthodox Church in the region. Protestant teachings promoting work and entrepreneurship as a virtue may also have been attractive in an area that cultivated the image of the "toiler" and hard physical labor. Protestants have targeted people in difficult life circumstances—people with drug and/or alcohol addictions, former prisoners, orphans, and dysfunctional families—and the life circumstances of some residents of the region were indeed difficult.[8] Finally, Protestants have found it somewhat easier to hold services and expand their own churches than Orthodox or Greek Catholics. Unlike the latter, who faced opposition from local authorities in the region when it came to allocating land for building a church or construction work, Protestants—citing Jesus's words in the Bible, "For where two or three gather in

---

5   Oleh Forostiuk, *Luhanshchyna relihiina: Istorychnyi i pravovyi aspekty* [Religion in the Luhansk region: Historical and legal aspects] (Luhansk: Svitlytsia, 2004).

6   Ibid.

7   Voinalovych and Kochan, *Relihiinyi chynnyk*, 206.

8   Although the number of penitentiary institutions in the region cannot be considered evidence in favor of the stereotype that Donbas is a land of crime and criminality, official statistics show that the Donetsk and Luhansk regions have the most prisons compared to other regions of Ukraine—20 and 16 respectively. For comparison, there are 7 penitentiary institutions in the Kyiv region, 6 in the Kherson region, and 5 in Crimea (183 institutions in total). *Perelik naimenuvan' organiv, ustanov vikonannia pokaran', slidchykh izoliatoriv Derzhavnoi kriminal'no-vykonavchoi sluzhby Ukrainy*, Ministerstvo iustitsii Ukrainy, May 10, 2017, https://minjust.gov.ua/n/22507.

my name, there am I with them"[9]—gather in so-called house churches, so they are less dependent on formal conditions for holding their services.

In the case of some other denominations, the civic identity of believers was closely interconnected with their religious identity, but the Protestants as a community did not have such a connection until 2014. Voinalovych and Kochan diplomatically note: "From an ethnopolitical point of view, Protestant organizations are characterized by an irrelevant attitude to issues of ethnicity and its essentialist markers."[10] In other words, Protestants tended to take a rather neutral position on political issues (referring to the words of St. Peter: "If you want to have a quiet and peaceful life, pray for those who are in authority!"[11]), and Protestant communities in the East were characterized by "local patriotism," whereby they interpreted changes in the state through changes in the situation of their congregation and in people's lives.[12] Similarly, the language issue was not on the Protestant communities' agenda at all—rather, Protestants in Donbas were in favor of preaching in a language that the congregation understood (which for most people was Russian), as opposed to the Church Slavonic used in the churches of the Moscow Patriarchate.

While Protestantism is a Western religious movement that originated and spread from Europe, Ukrainian Protestants maintained ties with both Western Protestant communities (particularly on the basis of the aforementioned missionary work) and Russian ones, particularly to preserve "traditional family values" and to resist the harmful (in the eyes of Protestants) influence of the West in this regard. While, for example, the pastor of the Good News Church in Slovyansk, Petro Dudnyk, claims that before the 2014 war most of the parishioners held pro-Ukrainian views, some religious scholars tend to believe that

---

9 Matthew 18:20 (NIV).

10 Voinalovych and Kochan, *Relihiinyi chynnyk*, 213.

11 Dmytro Durniev, "'Molit'sia za nynishniu vladu!', abo Iak vyzhyvaiut' relihiini konfesii v 'L/DNR'" ["Pray for those who are in authority!" or How religious denominations survive in the "L/DPR"], Hromadske, November 26, 2020, https://hromadske.ua/posts/molitsya-za-ninishnyu-vladu-abo-yak-vizhivayut-religijni-konfesiyi-v-ldnr.

12 A quote from an interview with Petro Dudnyk, pastor of the Good News Church, is particularly illustrative here: "A typical situation in a family looks like this: a child opens the door, the warped door of his apartment. He smells the stench of alcohol, he hears his father cursing his mother, his mother answers him, and the child thinks: 'How can I get into my room without being noticed?' Well, I'm exaggerating, but here I am drawing a picture. For me, patriotism and change are when something happens such that a child opens the door of his apartment, senses a delicious kitchen smell, and hears strange words, when his father says: 'Darling, can you hand me this?' And she answers: 'Yes, of course, how can I help you?' They continue to talk calmly. *This is a real change for me. This is patriotism* [italics mine—K.Z.]. This is why I live here." The book author conducted the interview in Slovyansk on June 16, 2021.

Protestants in the South and East of Ukraine did not support the Euromaidan (of course, these two statements are not mutually exclusive, as a "pro-Ukrainian stance" can be interpreted differently in different regions of Ukraine, and the latter is difficult to confirm or deny, since no separate surveys on the political orientations of Ukrainian Protestants have been conducted). It was the Russian aggression in Donbas that forced Protestants in the Ukrainian East to define their civic affiliation for the first time.

This happened not because Protestants immediately became hostile to the invaders—in an attempt to maintain their aforementioned position of neutrality, some churches continued to carry on as normal. On the contrary, the militants declared Protestants, along with other non-Orthodox denominations, to be their enemies, and this forced Protestant communities into opposition.[13] It is worth noting that the invaders persecuted Protestants not only "for their faith" but also for their property and resources: they took away their cars, set up their own headquarters and weapons depots in their houses of worship, etc.[14] For some communities, the murder of four Pentecostals in Slovyansk was the turning point after which it became impossible to maintain a neutral position. On June 8, 2014, "DPR" militants arrested and tortured the two older sons of the pastor of the Church of Christians of the Transfiguration of the Lord, Albert and Ruvym Pavenko, as well as two other deacons of this church, Viktor Brodarsky and Volodymyr Velychko.[15]

After the outbreak of Russian aggression, Protestant communities were at the forefront of the volunteer movement: they got people out of the Russian-occupied territories, supplied food for the Ukrainian military,[16] paid ransoms to release those held captive by the enemy in the occupied territories (regardless of the captives' political views[17]), and became military chaplains. For example, Petro Dudnyk, together with his fellow community members, evacuated 16,000 people from Russian-occupied territories.[18] According to Ruslan Skalun, a volunteer from Mariupol and parishioner of the Church of the Lord Jesus Christ who was quoted by the *NV* news outlet, Protestant communities were able to

---

13 Nataliia Sokolovs'ka, "Peresliduvannia na Donbasi" [Persecutions in Donbas], *Deutsche Welle*, August 10, 2014, https://p.dw.com/p/1Cs5O.

14 Durniev, "'Molit'sia za nynishniu vladu!'"

15 "Areshty, straty ta zakhoplennia khramiv: Okupatsiina vlada na Donbasi peresliduie virian" [Arrests, executions and seizures of churches: The occupation authorities in Donbas persecute believers], Zmina.info, October 25, 2018, https://zmina.info/news/areshti_strati_ta_ zahoplennjia_khramiv_okupacijna_vlada_na_donbasi_peresliduje_virjian/.

16 Shapoval, "Protestanty z Donbasu."

17 Ekaterina Sergatskova, "Istoriia pastora, kotoryi spasaet pastvu" [The story of a pastor saving his parish], *Ukrains'ka pravda. Zhyttia*, July 9, 2014, https://life.pravda.com.ua/ society/2014/07/9/174539/.

18 Shapoval, "Protestanty z Donbasu."

quickly pivot to volunteer work because they had an established infrastructure: the Renewal church in Mariupol gave the premises of its children's homes over to IDPs, and the hospice of the Church of Good Changes housed elderly people from the Joint Forces Operation zone.[19] At the same time, the war became an opportunity for Protestants to continue their missionary activities: Good News alone opened 28 missionary centers in frontline cities during the war, trying not only to provide humanitarian and spiritual aid but also to stimulate initiative and entrepreneurship among the local population—for example, by opening a bakery in frontline Mariinka.[20]

The policies of the "DPR" and "LPR" regarding Protestant churches that stayed in the occupied territories varied: in the "DPR" they could operate subject to "registration," while in the "LPR" most churches were denied "registration." According to Protestant pastor and volunteer Serhiy Kosyak, these differences demonstrate not so much different attitudes toward the churches as different methods of control over their work.[21] A number of churches that remain under occupation have had their property confiscated and have to rent premises to hold services, while the pastors preach via video link from Ukrainian-controlled territory.[22] Some have sided with the invaders: for example, the Gethsemane Church in Donetsk did not support the Prayer Marathon in 2014 and organized the supply of humanitarian aid from Russia.[23] At the time of writing (summer 2021), the church was still active in occupied Donetsk.[24]

Protestants active in the government-controlled territories of the Donetsk and Luhansk regions have good relations with other denominations (except for the Ukrainian Orthodox Church,[25] which represents the Russian Orthodox Church in Ukraine (formerly the Moscow Patriarchate)). They generally do

---

19 Ibid.
20 Bogdan Kinashchuk and Evgenii Savateev, "Vera vo vremia voiny. Kak konflikt na Donbasse izmenil protestantskuiu tserkov'" [Faith in times of war. How the conflict in Donbas has changed the Protestant Church], Hromadske, October 27, 2017, https://hromadske.ua/ru/posts/vera-vo-vremia-voiny-kak-konflykt-na-donbasse-yzmenyl-protestantskuiu-tserkov.
21 Iryna Slavins'ka, "Protestanty dlia okupatsiinoi vlady ie ideolohichnymy vorohamy,—sviashchenyk-volonter Serhii Kosiak" ["Protestants are ideological enemies for the occupation authorities," says pastor and volunteer Serhii Kosi ak], Hromadske Radio, June 4, 2019, https://hromadske.radio/podcasts/hromadska-hvylya/protestanty-dlya-okupaciynoyi-vlady-ye-ideologichnymy-vorogamy-svyashchenyk-volonter-sergiy-kosyak?fbclid=IwAR2_He4UyfSLAhA9eSfBSz5Go4arN_POSdiql0tDnDOabWjDMfGNrxaoxF4.
22 Durniev, "'Molit'sia za nynishniu vladu!'"
23 Ibid.
24 Gethsemane Church, Donetsk, https://www.facebook.com/groups/192074721449741/.
25 After Ukraine got the recognition of the autocephaly of the Orthodox Church of Ukraine, the Orthodox Church of Moscow Patriarchate insisted on calling itself "The Ukrainian Orthodox Church" to confuse its Ukrainian parishioners, without any acknowledgement of the ties to Russia in its title. On 20 August 2024 the Ukrainian Orthodox Church of the Moscow Patriarchate was officially banned by the Verkhovna Rada of Ukraine.

not compete with the Orthodox Church of Ukraine or the Greek Catholics for parish members and maintain partnerships with other religious communities, as well as with Protestant communities throughout Ukraine. According to Mykhailo Cherenkov, a professor at the Ukrainian Catholic University, the war is "a chance for Protestants to fit themselves into the Ukrainian identity."[26] This is true for at least some Protestants in the Ukrainian East.

Since the outbreak of the full-scale invasion, Gennadiy Mokhnenko and his fellow believers have evacuated about 1,800 people from Mariupol. Six of his sons are fighting in the Ukrainian armed forces, and one of his daughters was killed during the shelling of Mariupol.[27] He now serves as an army chaplain.

The Ukrainian Orthodox Church of the Kyiv Patriarchate: A Confrontation[28]

In 1991, Ihnatiy Volovenko enrolled as a first-year student at the Faculty of Philology of Donetsk University, majoring in Ukrainian language and literature. There, he became interested in folklore studies and Ukrainian rituals, including religious ones. One Easter, in the village of Zvanivka, he met a Greek Catholic priest and joined a small Greek Catholic community of up to twenty-five people in Donetsk, which, in the absence of a church of its own, gathered for services in some barracks. In 1994, the young man decided to enroll in the Greek Catholic seminary. However, his friends dissuaded him: "You know, the Greek Catholic Church is great and all that. But the church that Moscow is much more afraid of is the Orthodox Church of the Kyiv Patriarchate." In 1998, Father Ihnatiy was ordained as the third priest of the Ukrainian Orthodox Church of the Kyiv Patriarchate in the Donetsk region.

Since 1992, when the Ukrainian Orthodox Church of the Kyiv Patriarchate (UOC-KP) was established, the confrontation between the "national" church and the Moscow church has been unequal. As of January 1, 2011, the Ukrainian Orthodox Church of the Moscow Patriarchate (UOC-MP) accounted for

---

26 Kinashchuk and Savateev, "Vera vo vremia voiny."

27 Evhen Polozhii, "Mobil'ni krematorii, iaki rosiiany vykorystovuiut u Mariupoli,—tse suchasnyi mobil'nyi Oświęcim,—viiskovyi kapelan Gennadii Mokhnenko" ["The mobile crematoria Russia uses in Mariupol are a modern mobile Auschwitz," says military chaplain Gennadiy Mokhnenko], Censor.net, August 8, 2022, https://censor.net/ua/resonance/3357369/mobilni_krematoriyi_yaki_rosiyany_vykorystovuyut_u_mariupoli_tse_suchasnyyi_mobilnyyi_osventsim_viyiskovyyi.

28 Since the chapter deals with events before 2014, before the Tomos of autocephaly was granted by the Ecumenical Patriarch, the name "Ukrainian Orthodox Church of the Kyiv Patriarchate" is used instead of "Orthodox Church of Ukraine."

41.1% of all religious communities (86.8% of the total number of Orthodox communities) in the Donetsk region, while the UOC-KP accounted for 4.8%.[29] In the Luhansk region, the UOC-MP accounted for 51.0% of the total number of religious communities, while the UOC-KP accounted for 3.5%.[30] The Ukrainian Autocephalous Orthodox Church also had minimal representation in the region.

Here, in order not to mislead the reader, it is important to provide a certain "religious context" for the region: despite the widespread stereotype of the Donetsk and Luhansk regions as "fiefdoms" of the UOC-MP, the church of the Moscow Patriarchate had two powerful competitors: Protestant churches and atheism. In 2010, it was only in the Luhansk region (but not in Donetsk) that the UOC-MP had an absolute majority of all existing religious communities (50.4%)—for comparison, in the Chernihiv region, where the UOC-MP had the largest share of communities in Ukraine, that figure was 59.6%.[31] In the Donetsk region, the figure was only 40%, while Protestant communities accounted for 46%. In 2013, 12.1% of non-believers and convinced atheists lived in the East—the highest number compared to other regions—and another 21% of people hesitated between faith and atheism.[32] The fact that Orthodoxy was not so much a religious identity as a fetish, a simulacrum, for at least part of the population, is evidenced by the attitude to churches and religious symbols that manifested itself in local discourse. For example, local people in Donetsk sometimes referred to churches not by the names of their patron saints but by the names of the businessmen who had financed their construction: "This is Zvyahilsky's church, this is Rybak's, that one is Vyshnevetsky's."[33] Oleksandr

---

29 Voinalovych and Kochan, *Relihiinyi chynnyk*, 145.

30 Ibid.

31 "'Relihiia i vlada v Ukraini: Problemy vzaiemovidnosyn'. Informatsiino-analitychni materialy do Kruhloho stolu na temu: 'Derzhavno-konfesiini vidnosyny v Ukraini, ikh osoblyvosti i tendentsii rozvytku' 8 liutogo 2011 r." [Religion and power in Ukraine: Problems of relations." Information and analytical materials for a roundtable discussion on "Church-state relations in Ukraine, their features, and development trends," February 8, 2011], Tsentr Razumkova, Kyiv, https://www.razumkov.org.ua/upload/prz_2011_Rlg_smll.pdf.

32 Ibid.

33 Volodymyr Volovnenko, "'Metodom poslidovnoi liubovi', Arkhiiepyskop Donetskyi i Mariupol'skyi Serhii—pro sytuatsiiu v ieparkhii UPTs KP, plany na zavtra ta mrii 'na potim'" ["With the method of consistent love," Archbishop Serhiy of Donetsk and Mariupol on the situation in the diocese of the UOC-KP, plans for tomorrow, and dreams "for later"], *Den'*, May 30, 2013, https://day.kyiv.ua/uk/article/cuspilstvo/metodom-poslidovnoyi-lyubovi. Yukhym Zvyahilsky was Ukraine's MP from the first to the eighth Rada convocations, former member of the Party of Regions and the Opposition Bloc faction. Volodymyr Rybak was MP during the seventh convocation, one of the co-founders of the Party of Regions, and the Rada chairman in 2012–2014. Viktor Vyshnevetskyi is an entrepreneur from Donetsk region, owner of the Coal Energy holding, which includes several plants and mines.

Mykhed mentioned an example from Kostiantynivka, where churches were named not after businessmen, but after the names of the founders' enterprises— St. Konti's Church (Konti being a confectionery manufacturer), St. Vtormet's Church, St. Lead's Church, St. Megatex's Church[34]—and in Bakhmut, one of the streets where the mayor and his son built themselves mansions opposite "their" church is ironically called the Street of the Father, Son, and Holy Spirit.[35]

However, when any figures, absolute and relative, are compared, it becomes clear that there were only a few real UOC-KP churches and communities in cities and towns: 76 in the whole of the Donetsk region and 27 in the entire Luhansk region.

There are several reasons for the oppressed state of the UOC-KP in Donbas. First of all, the Kyiv Patriarchate in Donetsk and Luhansk has suffered from administrative and information-related pressure from the UOC-MP, which acted in unison with the local authorities. An example that speaks volumes is that while the UOC-KP managed to build one (!) church in the Donetsk and Luhansk regions in 1992–2010, and three were under construction, during the same period the Moscow Patriarchate had 219 churches and chapels built in the Donetsk region and 25 in the Luhansk region, and 68 and 18 churches respectively were under construction as of early 2011.[36] The UOC-KP held services in basements, trailers, and utility rooms that were converted into churches instead. Father Ihor, rector of the Church of Saints Borys and Hlib in Kramatorsk, recalled a visit by Patriarch Filaret to his former parish.[37] "Where is your church?" Filaret asked. "Here, in the basement," Father Ihor replied. "In the basement?" Filaret asked, upset. But when he went inside, he was pleasantly surprised: "Wow! I would never have believed that a church like this could be built in a basement."[38]

It was difficult to obtain or purchase a plot of land to build a church, as local authorities prevented the construction of churches, even if it was done at private expense.[39] For example, when the community tried to build a church in Druzhkivka, the construction was banned by order from Donetsk.[40] Instead,

---

34 Mykhed, I'll Mix Your Blood with Coal, 87.
35 Ibid, 62.
36 Voinalovych and Kochan, Relihiinyi chynnyk, 324, 329.
37 The Patriarch himself, by the way, is from the Donetsk region. He was born on January 23, 1929 in the village of Blahodatne, Amvrosiivka district.
38 The story is recorded from the words of Father Ihor, Kramatorsk, June 15, 2021.
39 "Otets' z ilovais'koho otochennia: Iak sviashchennyk Ihor Shemiakov riatuvav biitsiv i rozbu- dovuie parafii PTsU ta 'Plast'" [Father from the battle for Illovaisk: How priest Ihor Shemiakov saved soldiers and is building parishes of the Orthodox Church of Ukraine and 'Plast'"], Novynarnia, August 28, 2020, https://novynarnia.com/2020/08/28/ihor-shemiakov/.
40 Interview with Father Ihor, Kramatorsk, June 15, 2021.

churches of the Moscow Patriarchate were built with the assistance of local authorities and oligarchs, including Viktor Nusenkis, Vadym Novynskyi, and others.

Moreover, the UOC-MP waged a powerful information campaign against the UOC-KP (and not only in the Donetsk and Luhansk regions): churches, priests, and parishioners of the Kyiv Patriarchate were condemned as "schismatics" and supporters of a "non-canonical" Church. A well-known chapter in the history of the UOC-KP in the Donetsk region is the visit of Patriarch Filaret to Mariupol in 1999 to consecrate a cross on the site where a future church was to be built. At the site of the consecration, he and the priests who had accompanied him were met by men and women who attacked Filaret, and he and several other priests were injured.[41] Filaret's supporters accused the Moscow Patriarchate of organizing the attack. This was the most widely publicized story, but it was not the only occasion on which churches and priests of the Kyiv Patriarchate became the targets of aggression from both the local population and *titushky* (armed young men who were specially brought in)[42] when the local population (whether instructed to do so by the authorities or not) opposed the construction of Kyiv Patriarchate churches.[43]

The Kyiv Patriarchate was also chronically understaffed. There were frequent cases of priests serving in parishes without a proper theological education: in 2009, 64% (!) of priests in the Donetsk region had no relevant (theological) education, 25% of the clergy had secondary education, and only 11% had higher education, in contrast to the UOC-MP, where the vast majority of clergy had received secondary theological education.[44] Because of this, "random," untrained people sometimes became clergy, which undermined the authority of the church in the eyes of believers.[45]

At the same time, serving in Kyiv Patriarchate churches was not a very attractive prospect for "professional" priests—not only because of administrative pressure

41 "Kak v Mariupole izbivali Patriarkha Filareta. 20 let posle tragedii" [The assault on Patriarch Filaret in Mariupol. 20 years after the tragedy], 0629.com.ua, April 15, 2019, https://www.0629.com.ua/news/2363134/kak-v-mariupole-izbivali-patriarha-filareta-20-let-posle-tragedii-video; Volovnenko, "'Metodom poslidovnoi liubovi.'"
42 Liudmyla Klishchuk, "Ukrains'kyi khram na Donbasi: Sudy, krov ta moskovs'ki pohrozy" [A Ukrainian church in Donbas: Courts, blood, and threats from Moscow], Novynarnia, May 17, 2018, https://novynarnia.com/2018/05/17/ukrayinskiy-hram-na-donbasi-sudi-krov-ta-moskovski-pogrozi/
43 Volovnenko, "'Metodom poslidovnoi liubovi.'"
44 Even Father Serhiy (Horobtsov), who is now Archbishop of Donetsk and Mariupol of the Orthodox Church of Ukraine, was ordained a priest five years before he graduated from the Kyiv Theological Seminary.
45 Interview with a representative of the clergy in the Donetsk region, June 2021.

and resistance from local communities, but also because of the UOC-KP's modest financial capability. Compared to other influential denominations in the East—the UOC-MP, which had the support of government and oligarchic resources; Protestant churches that stimulated the spirit of entrepreneurship among their parishioners and encouraged them to make regular donations for the needs of churches and communities; and even the Ukrainian Greek Catholic Church (UGCC)—the UOC-KP has neither mastered the skills of effective fundraising nor acquired powerful patrons. UOC-KP priests have had to work in secular positions to support themselves and their families: for example, Father Ihnatiy taught at the Department of Religious Studies in Donetsk, Father Ihor repaired electrical appliances and worked as a taxi driver, and Father Volodymyr, who now serves in one of the few churches of the Orthodox Church of Ukraine in the occupied territory, works as a repairman at a Donetsk factory.[46] Due to the unfavorable conditions provided by the UOC-KP, it was difficult to retain young priests who came to the region by assignment from the Kyiv Theological Seminary,[47] and the church leadership concluded that it was best to recruit local priests who knew the region well and had a personal connection to it.[48] On the other hand, there are numerous cases of priests of the Kyiv Patriarchate beginning their career in the Moscow Patriarchate, either as ministers, such as the parish priest of the Holy Presentation Church in Kostiantynivka, Father Kostiantyn (Kuznyetsov),[49] or as parishioners.

However, it should be noted that despite the UOC-MP's numerical advantage in terms of churches and qualified personnel, the UOC-KP enjoyed some support among the population in the East. According to the Razumkov Center, the number of UOC-KP believers in the East was lower than that of the UOC-MP, but still significant (it is important to note that in these surveys, the "East" as a region includes, in addition to Donetsk and Luhansk, the Kharkiv, Dnipro, and Zaporizhzhia regions as well).[50] However, the most substantial category until

---

46 Durniev, "'Molit'sia za nynishniu vladu!'"

47 "Otets' z ilovais'koho otochennia."

48 "Iepyskop Afanasii (Iavors'kyi): Ne mozhna dopuskaty relihiinoi vorozhnechi na Luhanshchyni" [Bishop Athanasius (Yavorsky): There should be no room for religious hatred in the Luhansk region], Luhanshchyna.ua, February 14, 2020, http://luganskua.com/news/7345-episkop-afanasii-yavors-kii-ne-mozhna-dopuskati-religiinoi-vorozhnechi-na-luganshchini/.

49 Klishchuk, "Ukrains'kyi khram na Donbasi."

50 Forostiuk, *Luhanshchyna relihiina*, citing the sociological laboratory of the Luhansk Academy of Internal Affairs, presents even more optimistic figures for the UOC-KP: 40% of respondents in 2003 (and 42% in 1998) described themselves as believers of the Ukrainian Orthodox Church of the Kyiv Patriarchate.

2014 was those who called themselves "just Orthodox," meaning they did not favor either the Moscow or Kyiv Patriarchates.

Table 9. Which Orthodox Church do you belong to? (%)[51]

	2000	2010	2013	2014
Ukrainian Orthodox Church (Kyiv Patriarchate)	3.0	12.5	13	17.0
Ukrainian Orthodox Church (Moscow Patriarchate)	6.6	21.6	21.4	24.2
Ukrainian Autocephalous Orthodox Church	0.3	0.2	0.0	0.1
Just Orthodox	54.5	34.8	28.1	28.1
I don't know	5.1	0.6	2.0	1.7

Moreover, belonging to the UOC-KP did not mean parishioners were necessarily "pro-Ukrainian"—the attitudes of the Druzhkivka community of the Church of St. Seraphim of Sarov to the Euromaidan and the annexation of Crimea varied so much that the community split.[52] Parishioners of other UOC-KP churches could leave the parish if the priest's views on the occupation differed from theirs.[53]

Some UOC-MP priests and parishioners are supportive of Ukraine but do not express this publicly. Volodymyr Rafeyenko, who was a parishioner and bell-ringer at the Holy Transfiguration Cathedral (UOC-MP) in Donetsk, recalled how he and his fellow bell-ringers played "a kind of jazz in honor of Ukraine" on the church bells on July 5, 2014, when several thousand militants armed with weapons and heavy equipment entered Donetsk.[54]

After 2014, the UOC-KP in the occupied parts of Donetsk and Luhansk regions found itself in an "illegal status"—like other denominations, except for the Orthodox Church of the Moscow Patriarchate, it was persecuted, accused of

---

51 "Osoblyvosti relihiinoho i tserkovno-relihiinoho samovyznachennia ukrains'kykh hromadian: Tendentsii 2010–2018 rr. (informatsiini materialy)" [Particular features of the religious and church-religious self-determination of Ukrainian citizens: Trends in 2010–2018. Information Materials], April 26, 2018, Tsentr Razumkova, Kyiv, https://razumkov.org.ua/uploads/article/2018_Religiya.pdf.

52 Interview with Father Ihor, Kramatorsk, June 15, 2021.

53 "Otets' z ilovais'koho otochennia."

54 Volodymyr Rafeyenko, "It's Important to Understand that It Wasn't Regional Peculiarities that Caused This War, and It Wasn't the Ukrainians who Brought It On," in Mykhed, *I'll Mix Your Blood with Coal*, 319.

espionage and sabotage, its property was taken away, etc.[55] Prior to the full-scale invasion, some Ukrainian Orthodox priests had continued to serve in the occupied territories, mostly in rural churches[56] and/or underground, behind locked doors.[57] However, there are also openly pro-Ukrainian churches, such as the Holy Trinity Cathedral of the UOC-KP in Luhansk, whose Facebook page is still in Ukrainian and is regularly updated.[58]

In Ukrainian-controlled territory, the situation of the Orthodox Church of Ukraine (OCU), as the UOC-KP subsequently became known, improved somewhat after the onset of Russian aggression and the granting of autocephaly. For example, in 2015, the construction of a new church in Kostiantynivka, which had begun in the days of Viktor Yanukovych, was completed. The church had been intended for the UOC-MP, but after the Russian aggression, the church members changed their minds and decided that it would be the Holy Presentation Church of the Kyiv Patriarchate.[59] The subsequent lawsuit between the UOC and the OCU went on for several years.[60] In 2021, the Supreme Court of Ukraine ruled that the church would remain with the OCU.[61] But such situations are rather rare: in the Luhansk region, not one UOC-MP parish has officially gone over to the OCU.[62] It is still difficult to obtain land for the construction of a church, and churches in trailers are not uncommon.

As for Father Ihnatiy (Volovenko), when the Ukrainian Orthodox Church received the status of autocephaly from the Ecumenical Patriarch, he felt that he had fulfilled his mission. So he finally realized his plan: he became a Greek Catholic priest. In 2021, he served the Greek Catholic community in Bakhmut,

---

55 "U PTsU vidibraly khram na okupovanii teritorii Donets'koi oblasti" [OCU church seized in occupied territory of Donetsk region], Lb.ua, April 25, 2019, https://lb.ua/society/2019/04/25/425529_ptsu_otobrali_hram_okkupirovannoy.html; "Hlava UPTs KP zaiavliaie pro utysky virian na okupovanykh teritoriiakh Donbasu" [Head of UOC-KP claims harassment of believers in the occupied territories of Donbas], Zmina.info, April 30, 2018, https://zmina.info/news/glava_upc_kp_zajiavljiaje_pro_utiski_virjian_na_okupovanih_teritorijiah_donbasu/.

56 Durniev, "'Molit'sia za nynishniu vladu!'"

57 "Otets' z ilovais'koho otochennia."

58 Holy Trinity Cathedral of the UOC-KP, Luhansk, https://bit.ly/3Q916aR.

59 Klishchuk, "Ukrains'kyi khram na Donbasi."

60 After the Ukrainian Orthodox Church was granted autocephaly, the UOC-KP became known as the Orthodox Church of Ukraine (OCU), while the UOC-MP pretends to be a Ukrainian church by calling itself the Ukrainian Orthodox Church (UOC).

61 "Sviato-Stritens'kyi khram u prifrontovii Kostiantynivtsi zalyshaiet'sia v PTsU,—Verkhovnyi Sud" [Holy Presentation Church in frontline Kostiantynivka to remain in OCU, Supreme Court rules], Novynarnia, March 2, 2021, https://novynarnia.com/2021/03/02/svyato-stritenskyj-khram/.

62 "Iepyskop Afanasii (Iavors'kyi): Ne mozhna dopuskaty."

in the local Roman Catholic Church. In 2022, he witnessed the tragedy of occupied Irpin, where he had moved from Bakhmut.

The Ukrainian Greek-Catholic Church: Providence

The history of the revival of the Greek Catholic Church in the Luhansk region can hardly be described as anything other than Providence. In the 1950s, Hryhoriy Tsymbal, who belonged to a community of "true Orthodox Christians," was sentenced to fifteen years in a labor camp for "anti-Soviet activity," where he met Archbishop Josyf Slipyj of the Ukrainian Greek Catholic Church.[63] When he was released, Tsymbal became a committed Greek Catholic, continued his studies clandestinely, and in 1978 was ordained by Bishop Volodymyr Sternyuk, one of the leaders of the Catacomb Greek Catholic Church of Ukraine.[64] In 1992, Father Hryhoriy Tsymbal registered the first UGCC parish, Christ the King, in Luhansk.

The present-day Greek Catholic communities in Donbas were formed in two waves. The first wave was formed in 1951 by displaced persons—residents of several villages in western Ukraine who were brought to Donbas as a result of the Soviet-Polish exchange of territories (see Chapter 5). Boikos were relocated to the Bakhmut district of the Donetsk region and Lemkos to the Luhansk region. The Donetsk region's Boikos settled in three villages—Zvanivka, Rozdolivka, and Verkhnyokamianske. The second wave was represented by Galicians who had returned from exile and camps after Stalin's death and were forbidden to travel to western Ukraine, while the Ukrainian East offered jobs and easier adaptation in a "melting pot" of dozens of nationalities. In some places, there were so many people from western Ukraine that the Yasynivka Coke Plant in Makiivka was popularly dubbed "Bandera," for example, because of the large percentage of workers from western Ukraine.[65]

Under Soviet rule, Greek Catholics in the Ukrainian East were not able to openly practice their faith, but they preserved it until the restoration of independence (in part due to support from Greek Catholic priests from Galicia,

---

63 Father Hryhorii Tsymbal, *Tretia moskovs'ka spokusa (abo moi zustrichi z Patriiarkhom Iosyfom* [The third Moscow temptation (or My meetings with Patriarch Josyf)] (Lviv: Dzherela, 1997), 16–18.

64 Volodymyr Viatrovych et al., *Donbas: perePROchytannia obrazu* [Donbas: rereading the image] (Kyiv: Ukrains'kyi instytut natsional'noi pam'iati, 2018), 47.

65 Dmytro Bilyi, "Halychany na Donbasi: evolyutsiia identychnostei" [Galicians in Donbas: Evolution of identities], Zbruch, April 17, 2013, https://zbruc.eu/node/5911.

who would visit them on major religious holidays). Thus, the first official Greek Catholic parish in the Donetsk region was registered in Zvanivka in 1990, and the first priests to come to the East were fathers from the Congregation of St. Basil the Great (Basilian Fathers), including Father Myron Semkiv and several other young priests.

The number of Greek Catholics in the Ukrainian East is tiny: while Viktor Voinalovych and Natalia Kochan estimate it at 0.6% of the total population in the Luhansk region, a survey conducted as part of a Roundtable on "Church-State Relations in Ukraine in 2013" that covered the East as a whole found no UGCC parishioners at all (the 2010 figure was 0.8% of the population). Furthermore, according to the UGCC, in 2013 there were 33 Greek Catholic communities, one monastery, and a convent in the Donetsk region and four registered parishes in the Luhansk region with a total number of approximately 300 people.[66] As of early 2014, the publication *Nashe slovo* referred to six parishes in the Luhansk region: in Luhansk, Kreminna, Sievierodonetsk, Krasnyi Luch, and Antratsyt.[67] However, despite its small numbers, the Greek Catholic Church of the East is visible and active: for example, journalist Ruslana Tkachenko, visiting a Greek Catholic Church in Donetsk in the spring of 2014, noted that the church was not big enough to accommodate everyone wanting to attend the service, and Greek Catholic Father Tykhon (Serhiy Kulbaka) was one of the organizers of the Donetsk Prayer Marathon.[68]

The Greek Catholic Church remained strange and "Banderite" to the local authorities—yet the attitude towards it was not as hostile as towards the Orthodox Church of the Kyiv Patriarchate, as it was perceived as marginal, aimed only at a handful of people.[69] Still, it was very difficult to find a place to hold services or land for church construction. For example, it was not until 2010 that Luhansk parishioners were able to buy a house and turn it into a church; before that, they had to rent a room to hold the Divine Liturgy.[70] Nevertheless,

---

66 It is important to note that the number of communities and parishes is not equal to the number of churches, let alone priests. According to Father Vasyl Ivaniuk, as of 2021, there were up to 40 parishes (registered and unregistered) in the Ukrainian-controlled territory of the Donetsk region, served by just 13 priests.

67 "UHKTs v t. zv. 'LNR': Zavmerlo relihiine zhyttia" [UGCC in the so-called "LPR": Religious life has stalled], *Nashe slovo*, September 22, 2016, https://nasze-slowo.pl/ugkc-v-t-zv-lnr-zavmerlo-religijne-zh/.

68 Durniev, "'Molit'sia za nynishniu vladu!'"

69 This was only the perception of the local authorities, which did not correspond to reality. According to religious scholar Ihor Kozlovsky, the UGCC in the Donetsk region was the most popular of all the UGCC parishes on the Left Bank of the Dnipro.

70 Ibid.

the Greek Catholic fathers persistently went on developing new parishes and building churches, following the purely Galician principle of "don't wait, do it yourself."

Sometimes they even had to resort to deceit: for example, to buy land for a Greek Catholic church in Kramatorsk, Father Vasyl Ivaniuk, one of the young seminarians whom Myron Semkiv had invited to come to the region in the early years of independence, had to register it as private property, not church property. Later, in order to avoid pressure and threats while the church in Kramatorsk was being constructed, he had to build it in the village of Krynytsi, where he lived, and then dismantle it and transport it to Kramatorsk in parts. It was much easier to build a church in a village, a more inconspicuous and less public space, than in the city: in 1995, Father Vasyl acquired a partly built school from a collective farm in the Oleksandrivsk district of the Donetsk region, and he built a church on a section of its foundation.

After the Orange Revolution, the situation for the UGCC in Donbas improved somewhat, and it managed to obtain several plots of land for the construction of churches,[71] and even some ready-built churches: when Viktor Yushchenko became president, the Russian-speaking[72] (!) Greek Catholic parish of St. Andrew the Apostle in Donetsk acquired the right to use the "Cossack" interdenominational Church of the Nativity in the grounds of the Donetsk State University of Informatics and Artificial Intelligence. But when Viktor Yanukovych came to power, the local authorities' attitude toward Greek Catholics again became more critical: in particular, the Greek Catholics were forbidden to use the "Cossack" church. In Donetsk, the UGCC's cooperation with the charitable foundation Caritas, including projects aimed at helping homeless children and HIV-positive people, helped to establish relations with the local population and local authorities.[73] After 2014, Caritas in Kramatorsk became an important hub for helping the Armed Forces and displaced persons from the occupied parts of the Donetsk and Luhansk regions.

Greek Catholic priests admit that over time, and especially since the beginning of Russia's aggression in the East, the number of their parishioners has been in decline, primarily because many believers have left the region and new parishioners do not come as often: from the beginning of its work in Donbas,

---

71 "Nevidoma storona UHKTs na Donbasi" [An unknown side of the UGCC in Donbas], Ukrainian Greek Catholic Church website, March 26, 2014, http://news.ugcc.ua/interview/nevidoma_storona_ugkts_69844.html.

72 Despite its initial resistance to the use of Russian during services in the East, the UGCC eventually took a more moderate stance.

73 Ibid.

the Greek Catholic Church focused on meeting the spiritual needs of displaced Greek Catholics and their descendants rather than attracting new parishioners. Moreover, the Greek Catholic Church does not compete with other denominations: since the introduction of chaplains in the military, a Greek Catholic priest will recommend an Orthodox priest if an Orthodox soldier asks him to. Similarly, for example, all members of the Kramatorsk Council of Churches—in which only one Greek Catholic church is represented, and the majority are Protestant—have good working relations.

In the eyes of the Russian occupation authorities, Greek Catholics immediately became persona non grata: in 2014, Father Tykhon (Kulbaka) was held captive and tortured. Stepan Menko, the head of the Donetsk diocese of the UGCC, and several other priests were declared "particularly dangerous enemies" and "American spies."[74] At the same time, the UGCC does not hide the fact that Greek Catholic parishes remain and operate in the occupied territories with the permission of the occupying forces. Hryhoriy Tsymbal's work lives on: Father Mykola Yushchyshyn continues to serve in the Church of Christ the King. After 16 years of service in the Luhansk region, he was forced to leave when Russia's invasion of Ukraine began, but in 2015 he returned to Luhansk at the request of parishioners who had stayed in the temporarily occupied territory.[75] His church is also a refuge for some Orthodox and Roman Catholics who have been left without priests. [76]

Since February 24, 2022, Father Vasyl Ivaniuk has continued to work in the East as a military chaplain and head of the Caritas Foundation.

Muslims: A Choice

As a child, Said Ismagilov was given the Slavic name Serhiy. The register office employee insisted on it. But for Said, the name Serhiy remained only on paper. He is Said, a Muslim, an imam, a Tatar by birth, and a Ukrainian by citizenship.

The Islamic spiritual center where our conversation was to take place is located in Kyiv at 25A Dehtyarivska Street. It is a yellow high-rise building

74 Nataliia Kushnyrenko, "UHKTs u Donets'ku: Za khvoryi Donbas, proty ordy" [UGCC in Donetsk: For the sick Donbas, against the horde], Kurs, August 18, 2014, https://kurs.if.ua/articles/ugkts_u_donetsku_za_hvoryy_donbas_proty_ordy_4789.html/.

75 "Nastoiatel' parafii UHKTs rozpovsia iak povernuvsia do Luhans'ka popry zaboronu" [A UGCC priest tells the story of returning to Luhansk despite being banned], Hromadske radio, December 23, 2015, https://hromadske.radio/news/2015/12/23/nastoyatel-parafiyi-ugkc-rozpoviv-yak-povernuvsya-do-luganska-popry-zaboronu.

76 Ibid.

at the end of an alley with its own courtyard where children play: the center comprises a Muslim gymnasium (secondary school), a mosque, and the office of the "Ummah" Religious Administration of Muslims of Ukraine. The walls of Said's office are decorated with quotes from the Quran written in Arabic script. The Donetsk mullah talks to me in perfect Ukrainian. He looks stern, but he answers my questions in detail and in a friendly manner.

Despite the fact that Muslims make up only about 1.5% of the total diversity of religious faiths in the region,[77] Muslim communities have also played an interesting role in the history of Ukraine's Donetsk and Luhansk regions. After all, Donbas is the second-largest region in Ukraine after Crimea in terms of the size of the Muslim population and unique in terms of the activities of Muslim organizations (for example, the only Ukrainian Islamic University at that time operated in Donetsk from 1999 to 2002). Whereas in Crimea, Muslim communities were represented primarily by Crimean Tatars, in Donbas, they were primarily Volga Tatars, who were forcibly resettled from the Russian Volga region to develop Donbas industrially in the late nineteenth and early twentieth centuries.[78] But not exclusively: there are also some Muslims who moved to the region after Ukraine regained its independence, particularly people from Arab and other predominantly Muslim countries in the East—Syria, Yemen, Sudan, Palestine, Jordan, Algeria, Pakistan, etc.

After the Stalinist repressions of the 1930s (and in the case of the Crimean Tatars, after the deportation of 1944), Muslim communities in Ukraine existed underground and were only able to begin recovering in the late 1980s. In order to understand the landscape of Muslim organizations in the Ukrainian East, as well as the nature of their political orientation (in the sense of support or non-support for Ukrainian sovereignty and statehood), it is necessary to briefly explain the history of the revival of Muslim institutions in Ukraine in general. Two organizations were the first to emerge in independent Ukraine: the Spiritual Directorate of Crimean Muslims (SDCM) and the Spiritual Directorate of Muslims of Ukraine (DUMU). The latter, according to some observers, represents a tendency opposed to traditional Islam—Al-Ahbash.[79] Because of this, some Muslim communities in Ukraine did not join the DUMU.[80]

---

77 Voinalovych and Kochan, *Relihiinyi chynnyk*, 141.
78 Ibid., 246.
79 Bohdan Salhyrchuk, "Kudy ide musul'mans'ka umma Ukrainy pislia ahresii Rosii?" [Where is the Muslim Ummah of Ukraine headed after Russia's aggression?], *Den'*, July 31, 2016, https://day.kyiv.ua/article/polityka/kudy-yde-musulmanska-umma-ukrayiny-pislya-ahresiyi-rosiyi.
80 Ibid.

In eastern Ukraine, some Muslim communities have rallied around local oligarchs and criminal gang leaders of Tatar origin who are Muslim. In 1993, on the initiative of Akhat Bragin, Rashid Bragin, and others, the charter of the Muslim organization "Star of the Prophet" was registered in Donetsk, and in 1994, the foundation of the first mosque in the region, Ibn Fadlan, was laid with financial support from Bragin and later Rinat Akhmetov. After Bragin's assassination in 1995, the mosque was named in his honor, Ahat Jami.[81]

The role of Bragin and Akhmetov in the development of the Muslim community of the Ukrainian East did not end there—in 1994, Rashid Bragin was one of the founders of the Spiritual Center of Muslims of Ukraine (SCMU) with its headquarters in Donetsk, and in 1999, the Ukrainian Islamic University and—in violation of Ukrainian legislation prohibiting religious organizations from engaging in political activity—the Party of Muslims of Ukraine were established on the basis of the SCMU.[82] According to scholars, this party existed not so much to defend the rights of the Muslim minority as to serve as a tool of political struggle for the business elite of Donbas: to mobilize support from the Muslim community in favor of a local political force, as well as to oppose the Crimean Tatar Mejlis.[83] After all, in Ukraine, Muslims make up a relatively small but still significant share of voters—there is no exact estimate of how many people practice Islam in Ukraine, but researchers estimate up to 500,000 people in total (Islamic leaders estimate up to one or even two million people), of whom 30,000 to 200,000 live in the Donetsk and Luhansk regions.[84]

Politicians made no secret of their involvement in the work of the SCMU: when the Donetsk Mosque and the Ukrainian Islamic University were opened, the right to take part in the honorary opening was granted to Rashid Bragin, leader of the Party of Muslims of Ukraine, and Viktor Yanukovych, Head of the Donetsk Regional State Administration, along with the Istanbul Mufti.[85] In 2005, the Party of Muslims joined the ranks of the Party of Regions in its entirety.

The SCMU and the Party of Regions represented an influential, but not the only wing of Muslim communities in the Ukrainian East (Kuras National Academy of Sciences researchers Viktor Voinalovych and Natalia Kochan,

---

81 Ihor Kozlovs'kyi, "Svoieridnist' rozvytku islams'koho fenomenu v umovakh Donets'koho rehionu" [The distinctiveness of the development of the Islamic phenomenon in the conditions of the Donetsk region], *Ukrains'ke relihiieznavstvo* 3–4 (2004): 180, http://nbuv.gov.ua/UJRN/Ukrr_2004_3-4_22.

82 Voinalovych and Kochan, *Relihiinyi chynnyk*, 254.

83 Ibid., 254.

84 Ibid., 241.

85 Kozlovs'kyi, "Svoieridnist' rozvytku islams'koho fenomenu."

authors whom I cite extensively in this chapter, have noted that "it is inaccurate to speak of the Islamic community in Ukraine in the singular"). In addition to the SCMU, there were other Islamic organizations in Ukraine, and in the East in particular: the already mentioned Spiritual Administration of Muslims of Ukraine, the Kyiv Muftiate, whose leader was a member of the Council of Muftis of Russia,[86] the DUMU Ummah, which was formed from independent communities in 2008, the DUMU Yednannya, registered in 2012 with its governing center in Makiivka, and others. As of May 4, 2012, nine Muslim communities in the Donetsk region belonged to the SCMU and the DUMU, three communities to the DUMU Ummah, one community to the Kyiv Muftiate, and ten other communities were independent.[87]

The difference between these communities lay in the ethnicity of their members (indigenous Tatar ethnic groups and/or immigrant communities (Pakistanis, Afghans, Arabs, etc.)) and the external relations and support they sought. Among these external actors, three powerful centers of influence can be identified: Russia, Turkey, and the Middle East.

Given these trends, the Ummah Religious Administration of Muslims of Ukraine (the Ummah DUMU) was the only one that deliberately set out to develop Islam in Ukraine as a Ukrainian and European religious movement.[88] The pro-Ukrainian and pro-European vector of development was the factor around which the process of uniting some then-independent Muslim communities that did not want to join the existing spiritual directorates and centers began, particularly in 2007. Two of the five fundamental principles of the Ummah are as follows: "We are Muslims of Ukraine [. . .], part of the Ukrainian political nation and civil society [. . .]"; "Our vector is European. We believe that Ukraine is an integral part of the European cultural space. The Muslims of Ukraine are part of the Muslim Ummah of Europe."[89] It was this Administration that, according to Mykhailo Yakubovych, began the "Ukrainization" of Russian-language Islamic discourse in Ukraine (for example, its printed publication, *Ummah*, and Muslim literature were published in Ukrainian).[90] Ummah was not just the Administration of Muslims of the East: it brought together Muslim communities

---

86 Salhyrchuk, "Kudy ide musul'mans'ka umma Ukrainy."
87 Voinalovych and Kochan, *Relihiinyi chynnyk*, 258.
88 The full name of the organization is DUMU "Ummah." Hereinafter, "DUMU 'Ummah'" and simply "Ummah" are used interchangeably.
89 *Umma* 2 (September 2019): *Desiat' rokiv viry ta viddanosti* [Ten years of faith and devotion], https://www.calameo.com/read/00580584527eda9dc9ef6.
90 Mykhailo Iakubovych, *Vid Maidanu do ATO: Ukrains'ki musul'many v umovakh viis'kovopolitychnoi kryzy* [From Maidan to ATO: Ukrainian Muslims in the context of the military-political crisis] (Vinnytsia: Nilan, 2017), 36.

from all over Ukraine, with the center being in Kyiv. But the leadership of the DUMU Ummah was dominated by representatives of the Donetsk region.[91]

The Ummah was the only Muslim organization in Ukraine represented in the East that openly supported the Revolution of Dignity. On the night of December 1, the imams of the DUMU Ummah were traveling by train to a congress of communities at the Grand Mosque in Luhansk, and like most Ukrainian citizens, it was not until the next morning that they learned about the brutal beating up of students by police at Kyiv's Maidan. It was in that mosque that the imams of the Ummah issued a public appeal condemning the actions of the law enforcement bodies. Some of the imams were openly afraid to sign this appeal, some walked out during the signing—it seemed unthinkable and dangerous for some of them to openly condemn the actions of Viktor Yanukovych while in Luhansk. However, the majority of those present signed.

Later, the Ummah became one of the religious organizations in the East that, together with the Protestants, Greek Catholics, and Orthodox (Ukrainian Orthodox Church of the Kyiv Patriarchate), formed the religious wing of public resistance to the Yanukovych regime in Donetsk—in particular, it participated in the interdenominational Prayer Marathon and issued another statement regarding the January 18–20, 2014 shootings at the Kyiv Maidan. Said Ismagilov was a lecturer at the Open University of Maidan. The other Muslim organizations in Ukraine (except the DUMU) supported the Revolution of Dignity through participation in the activities of the All-Ukrainian Council of Churches and Religious Organizations, refraining from making individual statements.[92]

After the occupation of Crimea and Russia's aggression in the East in 2014, the DUMU and the DUMU Ummah remained active Muslim organizations in Ukraine. The mufti of the DUMU Yednannia positioned himself as the mufti of the "DPR,"[93] the Kyiv Muftiate has suspended its activities, and the communities of Rashid Bragin's Spiritual Center of Muslims of Ukraine have also adopted a pro-Russian position.[94] It is the Ummah, formally several times smaller than the DUMU,[95] that has essentially become the main organization of pro-Ukrainian Muslims: the Administration supports the Ukrainian-language website islam.

---

91 Voinalovych and Kochan, *Relihiinyi chynnyk*, 245.

92 Iakubovych, *Vid Maidanu do ATO*, 48.

93 Said Ismagilov et al., *Islam: Entsyklopedychnyi slovnyk* [Islam: An encyclopedic dictionary] (Kyiv: Vydavnytstvo Ruslana Khalikova, 2021), 148.

94 Durniev, "'Molit'sia za nynishniu vladu!'"

95 The DUMU has 150–160 registered communities, and the DUMU Ummah has approximately 30. However, Ismagilov insists that official statistics do not reflect reality and that the Ummah community is actually larger. So Salhyrchuk, "Kudy ide musul'mans'ka umma Ukrainy."

in.ua, and its representatives take part in academic conferences and public activities and give public interviews. After the outbreak of war, the Ummah established the Department of Military Chaplaincy of Muslims of Ukraine, registered with the Ministry of Defense, as well as the Eastern European Islamic University.

It is difficult to say exactly what the determining factor is in whether Ukrainian Muslims, at a certain point in their lives, take a pro-Ukrainian position or seek something else—neutrality or subordination to other countries. For Said Ismagilov, one of the main factors that influenced the formation of his identity as a Ukrainian was his studies in Moscow, at the Faculty of Theology of Moscow Islamic University, where he graduated in 2001 and received the title of imam. For four years, he frequently heard people say that the Ukrainian language, Ukrainian culture, and Ukrainians in general did not exist, and that Ukrainian independence was a joke. Such attitudes, as well as the authoritarian rule of Vladimir Putin and the persecution of Muslims in Russia, prompted Said to make a conscious choice in favor of Ukraine as a tolerant and democratic state.

In the spring of 2014, Said Ismagilov was still in Donetsk. In May 2014, he gave an interview to Donetsk journalist Tetiana Zarovna for the *Krayina* magazine in Donetsk's Al-Amal Mosque.[96] The title of the interview quoted his words: "I am surprised by my fellow Ukrainians who ask: 'What has Ukraine given me?' And what have you given it?" Said recalled that at the end of April 2014, he gathered the leaders of the communities of the Donetsk and Luhansk regions together and asked them: "Whose side are we on?" Everyone spoke unanimously: the spiritual administration was on the side of Ukraine.

Like many other pro-Ukrainian activists, Said Ismagilov had to leave Donetsk in September 2014: he had been warned ahead of time that he would be arrested. From then on, until Russia's full-scale invasion, he worked in Kyiv, but supported the communities that remained in Ukrainian-controlled territory in the Donetsk and Luhansk regions—in Sievierodonetsk, Kostiantynivka, Kramatorsk and Bakhmut.[97] Mosques stayed open in Sievierodonetsk, Luhansk region, and Kostiantynivka, Donetsk region.

---

96 Tetiana Zarovna, "'Dyvuiut' spivvitchyznyky, iaki kazhut': 'Shcho meni dala Ukraina?' A shcho ty zrobyv?" [I am surprised by my fellow Ukrainians who ask: 'What has Ukraine given me?' And what have you given it?], *Kraina*, May 6, 2014, https://gazeta.ua/articles/people-and-things-journal/_divuyut-spivvitchizniki-yaki-kazhut-so-meni-dala-ukrayina-a-scho-ti-zrobiv/556230.

97 Ummah communities also operate on the Russian-controlled territories of Donetsk and Luhansk regions. See the full list on the organization's website: "Hromady DUMU 'Umma,'" https://umma.in.ua/ua/gromady-dumu-umma.

The mosque in Sievierodonetsk served approximately 2,000 Muslims in the area, and its construction, sponsored by the community, began before the war and was completed in 2019.[98] Before the full-scale invasion, it was the main Ummah mosque in the Ukrainian-controlled area of Donbas. Its imam was Timur Beridze, an Adjarian by birth. He, like several other Ukrainian imams, is also a military chaplain, and supports fellow Muslims who serve in the Armed Forces.[99] The majority of Ukrainian Muslims remain in the occupied territories of Crimea and the East. Like other denominations that the "DPR" and "LPR" have labeled extremist, Muslims in the occupied territories are under threat and intense pressure: In 2018, Donetsk's only functioning mosque, Al-Amal, was closed after the imam and members of his congregation were searched and interrogated.[100]

After February 24, 2022, Said Ismagilov officially resigned from his position, and as of August 2022, he served as a paramedic in the Hospitallers medical volunteer battalion.[101] The new mufti is Sheikh Murat Suleymanov, the imam of the mosque of the Islamic Cultural Center of Lviv, a Crimean Tatar.

The mosque and the Bismillah Islamic Cultural Center in Sievierodonetsk were destroyed by Russian troops in July 2022. The mosque was shelled with cluster munitions. According to Said Ismagilov and Timur Beridze, Imam of Muslims in Sievierodonetsk and the Luhansk region, the shelling killed about 20 civilians who were sheltering in the mosque because they had access to water there (the community had a well).[102]

The mosque in Bakhmut, which was still under construction, was damaged by Russian shelling. As of August 2022, the mosque in Kostiantynivka was undamaged and open to the congregation.

98 Oleksii Vynohradov, "V Luganskoi oblasti vpervye s nachala konflikta na Donbasse otkryli mechet'" [Mosque opens in Luhansk region for first time since start of conflict in Donbas], Radio Svoboda, September 30, 2019, https://www.radiosvoboda.org/a/donbass-realii-mosque-in-severodonetsk/30191522.html.

99 Anastasiia Dashko, "'My vsi vid Boha': Iak ta za iakymy pravylamy zhyve musul'mans'ka hromada na Donbasi" ["We are all from God": How and according to what rules the Muslim community lives in Donbas], Vil'ne radio, January 27, 2021, https://freeradio.com.ua/my-vsi-vid-boha-iak-ta-za-iakymy-pravylamy-zhyve-musulmanska-hromada-na-donbasi/.

100 "Areshty, straty ta zakhoplennia khramiv."

101 At the time of the preparation of the book's English version (Fall 2024), Ismagilov is serving in the Armed Forces of Ukraine (author's note).

102 Said Ismagilov on Facebook, July 5, 2022, https://www.facebook.com/said.ismagilov.

An Almost-Afterword

Shakhtar Donetsk FC, Soccer, and the Role of Ultras in the Fight for the Country

In April 2014, an issue of the Italian magazine *Limes* came out with the title "Ukraine between us and Putin." One of the articles in it, covering the events of the Euromaidan, was titled "The Game of Ultras," and it contained the following sentence: "From the Carpathians to Donbas, dozens of soccer fans have joined the anti-Yanukovych protests and are fighting against Putin's goals, refuting the narrative that Ukraine is irredeemably divided between a pro-Russian East and a nationalist West."[1]

It should be noted that *Limes*, like Italian media discourse in general, does not have in-depth expertise on Ukraine. To reach such a heuristic conclusion—that Ukraine is not divided into two antagonistic parts, as Russian propaganda has been promoting for years—the Italians had to have been really touched by something. The key to the heart and mind of the writer was the story of Ukrainian soccer fans who supported the Revolution of Dignity with a united front. The role of fans from the East—Shakhtar Donetsk FC, Zorya Luhansk FC, Metalist Kharkiv FC, and Dnipro FC—was special in that outside observers, such as Italians who knew little about Ukraine but loved soccer, could see that this was about a goal that united the whole country.

---

1   Andrea Lucchetta, "La partita degli ultras, Ukraina tra noi e Putin," *Limes* 4 (2014).

In general, "conversion to Ukrainianness" in the East occurred mainly (though not exclusively) in two ways: through the family setting, when certain views and a certain culture were instilled in the family circle; and by traveling around Ukraine—through summer trips to visit a grandmother in the Khmelnytsky region, for example. In the case of the ultras, it was the traveling: fans went to matches all over the country and thus got to know not only other soccer fans but also Ukraine, and at the same time, as so often happens during traveling, became aware of their identity.

"My love for my football team grew into a love for my city, and then my country. I think that's how it should be," Oleksiy Chupa wrote in his unpublished novel *The Ways of St. James*[2] about Shakhtar Makiivka FC, which ceased to exist in 1998. For boys from small industrial towns, soccer was more than a passion, and sports stars were more than just role models. It was also a ticket to a better life, in the sense that the path to a dream does not necessarily lead to it, but helps to avoid hidden dangers. "We think back to all of our friends and realize that the group of us boys who were chasing a soccer ball around all day largely escaped what happened to our peers who were not interested in soccer. None of our guys went to jail or died of cirrhosis or drugs. And none of us is homeless. This gives me hope that we are still on the right track."

At some point, Shakhtar fans realized that the matches were not only about sports, but about politics too. As Vitaliy Ovcharenko, a Shakhtar fan since his student days, recalled, the ultras would not allow fans from Russia who came to support Shakhtar to hang the Russian flag in the stands: "Guys, we're friends, but this is Ukraine."[3] Shakhtar ultras would also protect fans from western Ukraine when they came to Donetsk to support their team, if someone was out to hurt them. A few years before the Revolution of Dignity and the start of Russian aggression, "moles" (an informal nickname for Shakhtar fans) spray-painted over billboards in Donetsk that were advertising the announcement of a Karpaty Lviv vs. Shakhtar Donetsk game with the slogan "West vs. East."

It was the ultras, who were skilled in self-defense and fistfighting, who stood up to defend Donetsk's Euromaidan when peaceful protesters were attacked by *titushky*. They wrote on their page on the social network *VKontakte*: "In view of the attack by *titushky* (January 22) on the local Euromaidan and the inaction of the police, Shakhtar fans decided to personally protect the people who came

---

2 Oleksii Chupa, "Dorohy Sviatoho Iakova" [The ways of St. James], in *Poroda. Antolohiia ukrains'ky kh pys'mennykiv Donbasu* [A rock: An anthology of Ukrainian writers of Donbas], ed. Veniamin Biliavs'kyi and Mykyta Hryhorov (Kyiv: Lehenda, 2017), 336.

3 Interview with Vitaliy Ovcharenko, January 26, 2021.

out to express their dissatisfaction with the authorities and lawlessness." They also emphasized: "We did not come to support the signing of the association [agreement] with Europe or to support the current corrupt opposition. We came to support our people as they fight for their rights. We want justice and a bright future. We are against the regime."[4]

But the two sides were too unevenly matched. The "moles" had hand-to-hand combat skills, but they could not counter the armature brought by the *titushky* and the armed police who supported the government. Moreover, the leadership of the very team they were supporting opposed the ultras.

Both Shakhtar FC and the Donbas Arena, built for Euro 2012, were controlled by Rinat Akhmetov, an oligarch close to Yanukovych and Ukraine's richest man, and the club's spokesman was Ruslan Marmazov (husband of the same Tetiana Marmazova who led the campaign against naming Donetsk National University after Vasyl Stus), who moved to Moscow in 2015. In the spring of 2014, several fans were banned from entering the stands for shouting "Putin is a d**khead." The ultras accused the Donbas Arena's security team of sharing their personal data with the Russian occupiers.[5] Thus, the fans were added to the lists of those who faced arrest and detention in the unrecognized "republics."

After the start of Russian aggression, the ultras continued to fight for Ukraine, some in the Armed Forces, others leaving the occupied territories as volunteers and in civilian jobs. In 2014, Maksym Lysenko, a Shakhtar fan from Pokrovsk, began making T-shirts featuring a picture of the rising sun and the slogan "Ukraine's Sun Rises in Donbas" to make the point that the Donetsk and Luhansk regions are Ukraine. This T-shirt was initially distributed among his fellow ultras, and then other Donetsk residents.[6]

***

---

4 "Ul'tras Shakhtaria zakhyshchaiut' donets'kyi Ievromaidan: My ne za opozytsiiu, my protu rezhymu" [Shakhtar ultras defend Donetsk's Euromaidan: 'We are not for the opposition, we are against the regime'], Texty, January 24, 2014, https://texty.org.ua/fragments/51237/ Ultras_Shahtara_zahyshhajut_doneckyj_Jevromajdan_my_ne-51237/.

5 Daniil Vereitin, "'Shahter' i ul'tras snova porugalis': Kto prav?" [Shakhtar and ultras quarrel again: Who's right?], Tribuna, March 5, 2019, https://ua.tribuna.com/tribuna/blogs/danilos/ 2368536/.

6 "Prynt, shcho h riie dushu donechchan: Iak iunak z Pokrovs'ka stvoryv naivpiznavanishyi symvol patriotychnogo Skhodu" [A heart-warming print for Donetsk residents: how a young man from Pokrovsk created the most recognizable symbol of the patriotic East], Vchasno. ua, July 1, 2019, https://vchasnoua.com/news/prynt-shcho-hriie-dushu-donechchan-iak-iunak-z-pokrovska-stvoryv-naivpiznavanishyi-symvol-patriotychnoho-skhodu.

In 2017, another conflict broke out between Shakhtar FC and its fans. During the last game in the Premier League, the club forbade the children of Ukrainian soldiers who were leading the teams out onto the pitch to wear shirts that said: "My father is a hero of Ukraine."[7] Fans blocked the club's bus and demanded explanations.

***

"Which soccer team do you support now?" I asked Vitaliy Ovcharenko.

He looked at me as if I had just said something stupid.

"Your question is completely inappropriate. You didn't stop loving Ukraine during Yanukovych's presidency, right?"

"No, I didn't."

"Well, I didn't stop loving Shakhtar either. Shakhtar was here before Akhmetov, and it will be here after Akhmetov."

***

In April 2022, Shakhtar Donetsk FC played against the Greek team Olympiacos FC wearing shirts that bore the names of Ukrainian hero cities— Mariupol, Irpin, Bucha, Hostomel, Kharkiv and so on—instead of their own names. Later, they also played in shirts featuring images of four-year-old Alisa, who at that time had been at the Azovstal steelworks in Mariupol for more than two months, and three-month-old Kira from Odesa, who was killed by a Russian missile along with her mother and grandmother.

***

Since the beginning of the full-scale invasion, Vitaliy Ovcharenko, an ATO veteran, has been defending Ukraine in the Armed Forces.

---

7 "Ul'trasy zmusyly 'Shakhtar' vyity na pole u futbolkakh na pidtrymku ukrains'kykh viis'k-ovykh" [Ultras force Shakhtar to come out in T-shirts in support of the Ukrainian military], TSN, November 21, 2017, https://www.youtube.com/watch?v=5qvClp4bdNA.

Afterword

In a Train Compartment with People from Donetsk, or Where Ukraine's Sun Rises

The Kostiantynivka–Kyiv train. May 2021.

I'm sharing a train compartment with my Donetsk friends and listening silently. I'm taking in their conversation: they're talking about the university where they studied back in Donetsk; about mutual acquaintances (some of whom are no longer with us); about colleagues—those who left and those who stayed "there"; they mention towns and villages, some of which have become familiar to all Ukrainians (Khartsyzk, Alchevsk, Rubizhne, Popasna, Volnovakha . . .), and some known only to locals; they use local words like *tormozok*, which means a lunch box ("I used to take a *tormozok* to school").

This conversation is just like any other train chatter between people with a shared past. Only for them, this past is Atlantis: although it exists in real time and space, it has very little in common with the one they remember.

***

"If I had to leave my city forever, I would be heartbroken," I said to Inna, my new friend who had left Luhansk and was living in Sievierodonetsk at the time. It was May 2021. "You only think that now," she replied. "You'd get used to it." "Aren't you afraid?" I asked. "The front line is only forty kilometers [twenty-five miles] away." "No. We make sure that we have all the essentials ready and the gas tank in the car is full. It's more like, when I see that something is brewing, I think: do I really have to go away somewhere again?"

At the time, I could not have even imagined that just nine months later I would be forced to leave Kyiv and become an IDP—an internally displaced person. An abbreviation that for eight years was used only for people from Donbas.

***

What future lies ahead for the Donetsk and Luhansk regions? When will the occupied territories become part of sovereign Ukraine again?

The answers to these questions will depend on the capabilities of the Ukrainian Armed Forces, the situation in Russia, and Western support for Ukraine, and each of these components has many unknowns. But the stance of most Ukrainians is clear: according to a poll conducted by the Kyiv International Institute of Sociology in July 2022, eighty-four percent of Ukrainians believe that no territorial concessions are acceptable to achieve peace with Russia.[1]

This opinion is understandable: after all, Russia's full-scale invasion has demonstrated that the Donetsk and Luhansk regions were never its main goal. So "giving up Donbas," as some have suggested, would not only mean Ukraine was willing to cede sovereignty and territory whenever Russia invades: it would also create a bigger foothold for Russia to continue its offensive.

Similarly, a so-called "frozen conflict" (an incorrect term, since it is not the conflict that is frozen but its solution) might stop the bloodshed for a while (in fact, this was the main reason Ukraine agreed to sign the Minsk agreements in 2015), but it would not prevent a bigger war.

Ukraine's goal is the full restoration of its territorial integrity within internationally recognized borders, and, at some point in the future, the reintegration of the occupied territories will appear on the agenda.

However, it is important to understand that the starting point for any discussion of the modality of Donbas integration (which includes disarmament, court trials and sentences for criminals, amnesty, democratic elections and the ability to participate in them, etc., not to mention the cost of reconstruction) should

---

1   "Dynamika h otovnosti do terytorial'nykh postupok dlia iaknaishvydshoho zavershennia viiny: Rezul'taty telefonnoho opytuvannia, provedenoh o 6–20 ly pnia 2022 roku" [Dynamics of readiness for territorial concessions to end the war: Results of a telephone survey conducted on July 6–20, 2022], Ky ivs'kyi mizhnarodnyi instytut sotsiolohii, https://www.kiis.com.ua/?lang=ukr&cat=reports&id=1124.

be the idea that in the event of the reintegration of the Donetsk and Luhansk regions, there are at least three dimensions that need to be taken into account.[2]

The first dimension is the occupied territories, which as of February 23, 2022, accounted for about 30% of the Donetsk and Luhansk regions. Prior to the full-scale invasion, it was estimated that between 1.6 million (Ukraine's version) and 2.8 million (UN estimates) people lived there.[3] After the full-scale invasion, this number fell due to the forced mobilization of the male population of the occupied territories and migration outside the Russian-occupied territories of Ukraine. The civilian population in these territories may remain loyal to the "authorities" of the "DPR"/"LPR" and/or Russia (I am not referring to collaborators here, who should be prosecuted for their crimes). Nevertheless, it is important to remember that these territories are still home to people with a pro-Ukrainian stance. I can't tell you how many of them are out there. But I have reliable evidence that such people are still there. Here are a few examples.

The Donbas Realities project, which Radio Svoboda has been running since the beginning of Russia's invasion in 2014, states the following: "We work on both sides of the contact line. If you live in the Russian-occupied territories of Ukraine and want to share your story, please write to us at Donbas_Radio@rferl.org or on Facebook, or call our answering machine. Your name will not be disclosed." Radio Svoboda journalists say they receive messages all the time. Some people thank them for not forgetting about those who stayed in the Russian-controlled territories. Others try to pass on some information. Since the beginning of the full-scale invasion, Radio Svoboda (and others) have received reports from the occupied territories about the location and movement of enemy units.

Here's another example: on January 24, 2022, the media outlet Reporters published a story called "We are here. How young people in the occupied territory of Donbas are fighting for Ukraine."[4] There has been quiet resistance during all the years of Russian occupation: young people have painted Ukrainian flags and coats of arms, organized short silent campaigns, etc.

---

2   These three dimensions are borrowed from Maksym Vikhrov's book *The Wild East*. However, Maksym Vikhrov mentions four dimensions: he also includes the "gray zone" between the Ukrainian-controlled (as of 2018) part of Donbas and the Russian-occupied territories.

3   Stanislav Asieiev, "ORDLO v tsyfrakh: chy ie koho povertaty?" [The Russian-occupied territories in numbers: is there anyone to bring back?], Radio Svoboda, March 17, 2021, https://www.radiosvoboda.org/a/donbas-ordlo-v-tsyfrakh/31151759.html

4   Ol'ha Omel'ianchuk, Lidiia Holosko, "My ie. Iak molod' na okupovanii chastyni Donbasu boret'sia za Ukrainu" [We are here. How young people in the occupied territory of Donbas are fighting for Ukraine], *Reporters*, January 24, 2022, https://reporters.media/tykhyi-sprotyv/?fbclid=IwAR0s50qHT3taQuYD5jj0xPbey9d-kxkTSPTWL1xCzToM_QOS_Suhqw4k7ys.

How many people are there who have something to say but have to stay silent? How many are there who stayed to "greet Ukrainian soldiers with flowers"[5] and to make sure that "there are still Ukrainians there"?[6]

The second dimension of Donbas is the Ukrainian-controlled territories of the Donetsk and Luhansk regions, which have undergone significant transformations over the past eight years. Some of these territories have been occupied since February 24, 2022, but their informational, social, and infrastructural background is significantly different from what it was in 2013 or early 2014. This is not only and not even so much about the political dimension, although the political dimension is important as well (in 2020 and 2021, Mariupol, for example, topped the Transparency and Accountability Ranking compiled by Transparency International Ukraine and was a beacon of the Azov region): this is also about the level of civil society. Since 2014, civil society in the Donetsk and Luhansk regions had developed exponentially, establishing more NGOs, hubs, and creative spaces than in some other regions of Ukraine that had not been ravaged by war (until February 24). "Vilna Khata" in Kostiantynivka, "Tochka Dostupu" in Druzhkivka, the Anti-Crisis Media Center in Kramatorsk, and the Eastern Ukrainian University, which moved from occupied Luhansk to Sievierodonetsk, are just some of the centers and spaces that had emerged since 2014.

The third dimension is that of the internally displaced people, those who left the Donetsk and Luhansk regions as a result of Russia's aggression in 2014 and 2022. After Russia's 2014 invasion, approximately 2 million people left the occupied territories of the Donetsk and Luhansk regions, 1.5 million of whom settled across Ukraine, from Kramatorsk, Sievierodonetsk, and Kharkiv to Chernivtsi and Uzhhorod. In fact, most of the people featured in this book belong to this dimension. And despite the fact that they are currently unable to return to their cities, are they not their legitimate representatives no less than those who (for various reasons) have remained in occupation?

---

5 "Kazaty 'Donbas'—pidtrymuvaty radians'kyi mif,—pys'mennytsia Olena Stiazhkina" ["To say 'Donbas' is to support the Soviet myth," says writer Olena Stiazhkina], Svoi.city, August 20, 2021, https://svoi.city/articles/160445/kazati-donbas-pidtrimuvati-radyanskij-mif--pismennicya-olena-styazhkina.

6 "'Koly chuiesh pershyi vybukh, ty maiesh sisty v mashynu i poikhaty, khoch by iak strashno bulo'. Istoriia Svitlany Kolodii z tsyklu 'Vnutrishnia mih ratsiia" ["Once you hear the first explosion, you have to get in the car and drive away, no matter how scared you are." The story of Svitlana Kolodiy from the "Internal Migration" series], Divoche.media, August 4, 2022, https://divoche.media/2022/08/04/pershyj-vybuh-ty-mayesh-sisty-v-mashynu-i-poyihaty-hoch-by-yak-strashno-bulo-istoriya-svitlany-kolodij-z-czyklu-vnutrishnya-migracziya/.

The Donetsk and Luhansk regions are acquiring new meanings and connotations both in the public consciousness and in the historical memory that is currently being formed. This region is where a new Ukrainian heroic myth is being created. In a few months of valiant defense, the Azovstal plant in Mariupol was transformed from a target of criticism for air pollution into a symbol of Ukrainian resilience. While the slogan "Donbas is Ukraine" was relevant in 2014, the mental shift of 2022 took place on an entirely different level. When, in April 2022, Russia dropped phosphorous bombs on Mariupol and carried out fifty airstrikes, Svyatoslav Palamar, the deputy commander of the Azov regiment, posted on his Telegram channel: "Today I won't say Mariupol is Ukraine; today I will say that Ukraine is Mariupol."[7] Ukraine's sun does rise in Donbas[8]—this romantic and well-known expression has suddenly acquired a new, poignant meaning.

The history of the Ukrainian East demonstrates what this region has suffered from Russia every time it has tried to forge an alternative trajectory of development. And the stories in this book confirm what it could have been if not for Russian interference; if it had had the "ten years" the people featured in this book talked about.

These stories illustrate what the Ukrainian East can still become.

---

7 MRPL on Facebook, April 28, 2022, https://www.facebook.com/watch/?v=1222638428567012.

8 This expression is an interpretation of the flag of the Donetsk region. It depicts a yellow sun against a blue sky, rising over a black field, a symbol of the Donetsk coal basin. The flag was approved in 1999.

   This book also has an alternative title, *Radiance and Testimony. Stories of the Ukrainian East of the Early Twenty-First Century*. It was suggested by Oleksiy Chupa when I tried to explain the gist of my research to him: "You know, this is a radiant book about a radiant region." I liked his suggestion, not only because of its postmodernism—a character in a book coming up with the title—but also because it was yet another argument supporting the idea of Ukrainian Donbas.

   Svitlo i spovid', or "Radiance and Testimony," is the title of an album by Taras Chubai, which means that, in the early 2000s, boys and girls in Makiivka, Zhytomyr, and Frankivsk were all listening to the same music.

Key Sources

Aseyev, Stanislav. *In Isolation: Dispatches from Occupied Donbas.* Translated by Lidia Wolanskyj. Cambridge: Harvard University Press, 2022.

Bilets'kyi, Volodymyr, et al. *My ydemo!: narysy z istorii Donets'koho oblasnoho tovarystva ukrains'koyi movy im. T. H. Shevchenka—pershoi masovoi natsional'no-demokratychnoi hromads'koi orhanizatsii Donechchyny.* [We're coming!: Essays on the history of the Taras Shevchenko Donetsk regional society of the Ukrainian language, the first major national democratic public organization in Donetsk region]. Donetsk: Skhid, 1998.

"Donbas Studies." Izolyatsia Foundation. https://izolyatsia.org/ua/project/donbas-studies.

Fedorchuk, Stanislav. *Demontazh lytsemirstva. Statti* [Dismantling Hypocrisy. Essays]. Kyiv: Smoloskyp, 2012.

———. *Slukhaiuchy symfoniiu Donbasu* [Listening to the symphony of Donbas]. Kyiv: Tempora, 2012.

Kazans'kyi, Denys, and Maryna Vorotyntseva. *Iak Ukraina vtrachala Donbas* [How Ukraine was losing Donbas]. Kyiv: Chorna hora, 2020.

Kul'chyts'kyi, Stanislav, and Larysa Yakubova. *Trysta rokiv samotnosti: ukrains'kyi Donbas u poshukakh smysliv i Bat'kivshchyny* [Three hundred years of solitude: Ukrainian Donbas in the search for meaning and homeland]. Kyiv: Klio, 2016.

Kuromiya, Hiroaki. *Freedom and Terror in the Donbas. A Ukrainian-Russian Borderland, 1870s–1990s.* Cambridge: Cambridge University Press, 2003.

Mykhed, Oleksandr. *I'll Mix Your Blood with Coal: Snapshots from the East of Ukraine.* Translated by Tetiana Savchynska and David Mossop. Evanston: Northwestern University Press, 2025.

Studenna-Skrukwa, Marta. *Ukrains'kyi Donbas. Oblychchia rehional'noi identychnosti* [Ukrainian Donbas. The Faces of Regional Identity]. Kyiv: Laboratoriia zakonodavchykh initsiatyv, 2014.

Vikhrov, Maksym. *Dykyi skhid. Narys istorii ta s'ohodennia Donbasu* [Wild east. Sketches on the past and present of Donbas]. Kyiv: Tempora, 2018.

Publications of the National Academy of Sciences of Ukraine

Dziuba, Ivan. *Donets'ka rana Ukrainy: Istoryko-kul'turolohichni esei* [The Donetsk wound of Ukraine: Historical and cultural essays]. Kyiv: Natsional'naia akademiia nauk Ukrainy, 2015.

Karmazina, Mariia. *Politychni identychnosti v suchasnii Ukraini: miska hromada Donetska.* [Political identities in modern Ukraine: Donetsk urban community]. Kyiv: Instytut politychnykh i etnonatsional'nykh doslidzhen' imeni I. F. Kurasa Natsional'noi akademii nauk Ukrainy, 2016.

Voinalovych, Viktor, and Nataliia Kochan. *Relihiinyi chynnyk etnopolitychnykh protsesiv na Donbasi: Istoriia i suchasnist'* [The religious factor in ethnopolitical processes in Donbas: History and present]. Kyiv: Instytut politychnykh i etnonatsional'nykh doslidzhen' imeni I. F. Kurasa Natsional'noi akademii nauk Ukrainy, 2014.

The Ukrainian East in Fiction

Biliavs'kyi, Veniamin, and Mykyta Hryhorov, ed. *Poroda. Antolohiia ukrains'ky kh pys'mennykiv Donbasu* [A rock: An anthology of Ukrainian writers of Donbas]. Kyiv: Lehenda, 2017.

Chupa, Oleksii. *Kazky moho bomboskhovyshcha* [Tales from my bomb shelter]. Kharkiv: Klub simeinoho dozvillia, 2015. [And other books by the author.]

Ivaniuk, Oleksandra. *Amor[t]e.* Chernivtsi: XXI, 2017. [A fictionalized retelling of Yuriy Matushchak's story.]

Yakimchuk, Lyuba. *Apricots of Donbas*. Translated by Oksana Maksymchuk, Max Rosochinsky, and Svetlana Lavochkina. New York: Lost Horse Press, 2021.

Zhadan, Serhiy. *Voroshilovgrad*. Translated by Reilly Costigan-Humes and Isaac Wheeler. Dallas: Deep Vellum Publishing, 2016. [And other books by the author.]

Must-watch Films

Eurodonbas (2022), directed by Kornii Hrytsiuk.
Symfoniia Donbasu (1930), directed by Dziga Vertov.